I0165790

POEMS (1786)

BY

Helen Maria Williams

TO HER MAJESTY.

MADAM,

I am too sensible of the distinguished honour conferred upon me, in your Majesty's gracious protection of these Poems, to abuse it by adopting the common strain of dedication.

That praise corresponds best to your Majesty's generous feelings, which is poured without restraint from the heart, and is repeated where you cannot hear.

I suppress therefore, in delicacy to those feelings, the warmth of my own, and subscribe myself,

MADAM,

With profound respect,

Your MAJESTY'S

Devoted servant,

HELEN MARIA WILLIAMS.

PREFACE.

The apprehension which it becomes me to feel, in submitting these Poems to the judgment of the Public, may perhaps plead my excuse, for detaining the reader to relate, that they were written under the disadvantages of a confined education, and at an age too young for the attainment of an accurate taste. My first production, the Legendary Tale of Edwin and Eltruda, was composed to amuse some solitary hours, and without any view to publication. Being shewn to Dr. Kippis, he declared that it deserved to be committed to the press, and offered to take upon himself the task of introducing it to the world. I could not hesitate to publish a composition which had received the sanction of his approbation. By the favourable reception this little poem met with, I was encouraged still farther to meet the public eye, in the "Ode on the Peace," and the poem which has the title of "Peru." These poems are inserted in the present collection, but not exactly in their original form. I have felt it my duty to exert my endeavours in such a revision and improvement of them, as may render them somewhat more worthy of perusal. It will, I am afraid, still be found, that there are several things in them which would shrink at the approach of severe criticism. The other poems that now for the first time appear in print, are offered with a degree of humility rather increased than diminished, by the powerful patronage with which they have been honoured, in consequence of the character given of them by partial friends. Knowing how strongly affection can influence opinion, the kindness which excites my warmest gratitude has not inspired me with confidence.

Poems (1786)

Helen Maria Williams

Contents

PREFACE. 8

AN AMERICAN TALE. 10

SONNET, To MRS. BATES. 15

SONNET To TWILIGHT. 16

TO SENSIBILITY. 17

A SONG. 21

AN ODE ON THE PEACE. 23

EDWIN AND ELTRUDA 36

A LEGENDARY TALE. 36

A HYMN. 52

PARAPHRASES FROM SCRIPTURE. 54

ISAIAH xlix. 56

MATT. vii. 59

AN EPISTLE TO DR. MOORE. 61

AN EPISTLE TO DR. MOORE, ...62

PART OF AN IRREGULAR FRAGMENT, FOUND IN A DARK PASSAGE ....
    OF THE TOWER. 71

ADVERTISEMENT. 71

PART OF AN IRREGULAR FRAGMENT, FOUND IN A DARK PASSAGE ....
    OF THE TOWER. 73

PERU. A POEM, IN SIX CANTOS. 82

ADVERTISEMENT. 84

THE ARGUMENT. 84

PERU. CANTO THE FIRST. 85

PERU. CANTO THE SECOND. 92

PERU. CANTO THE SECOND. 92

PERU. CANTO THE THIRD. 98

PERU. CANTO THE THIRD. 98

PERU. CANTO THE FOURTH. 105

PERU. CANTO THE FOURTH. 105

PERU. CANTO THE FIFTH. 112

PERU. CANTO THE FIFTH. 112

PERU. CANTO THE SIXTH. 124

PERU. CANTO THE SIXTH. 125

SONNET, ...137

QUEEN MARY'S COMPLAINT. 138

EUPHELIA, AN ELEGY. 141

SONNET, To EXPRESSION. 147

*   *   *   *   *

When I survey such an evidence of the zeal of my friends to serve me, as the following honourable and extensive list affords, I have cause for exultation in having published this work by subscription. They who know my disposition, will readily believe that the tear which fills my eye, while I thank them for their generous exertions, flows not from the consideration of the benefits that have arisen from their friendship. It is to that friendship itself, that my heart pays a tribute of affection which I will not attempt to express--for my pen is unfaithful to my purpose.--While I am employed in testifying my thankfulness for the favours I have received, it is impossible that I should forget how much I owe to one Gentleman in particular, whose exertions in my behalf, though I was a stranger to him, have been so marked, so generous, and indeed so unexampled, that it is a very painful task which his delicacy has imposed upon me, in not permitting me to mention his name. But such goodness cannot be concealed. The gratitude of my own heart has proclaimed it to my private friends; and the noble and honourable subscribers his zeal has procured, cannot avoid being sensible to whom I am indebted for so illustrious a patronage.

AN AMERICAN TALE.

"Ah! pity all the pangs I feel,
  If pity e'er ye knew;--
An aged father's wounds to heal,
  Thro' scenes of death I flew.

Perhaps my hast'ning steps are vain,
  Perhaps the warrior dies!--
Yet let me sooth each parting pain--
  Yet lead me where he lies."

Thus to the list'ning band she calls,
  Nor fruitless her desire,
They lead her, panting, to the walls
  That hold her captive sire.

"And is a daughter come to bless
  These aged eyes once more?
Thy father's pains will now be less--
  His pains will now be o'er!"

"My father! by this waining lamp
  Thy form I faintly trace:--
Yet sure thy brow is cold, and damp,
  And pale thy honour'd face.

In vain thy wretched child is come,
  She comes too late to save!
And only now can share thy doom,
  And share thy peaceful grave!"

Soft, as amid the lunar beams,
  The falling shadows bend,
Upon the bosom of the streams,
  So soft her tears descend,

"Those tears a father ill can bear,
  He lives, my child, for thee!
A gentle youth, with pitying care,
  Has lent his aid to me.

Born in the western world, his hand
  Maintains its hostile cause,
And fierce against Britannia's band
  His erring sword he draws;

Yet feels the captive Briton's woe;
  For his ennobled mind,
Forgets the name of Britain's foe,
  In love of human kind.

Yet know, my child, a dearer tie
  Has link'd his heart to mine;
He mourns with Friendship's holy sigh,
  The youth belov'd of thine!

But hark! his welcome feet are near--
  Thy rising grief suppress--
By darkness veil'd, he hastens here

To comfort, and to bless."--

"Stranger! for that dear father's sake
  She cry'd, in accents mild,
Who lives by thy kind pity, take
  The blessings of his child!

Oh, if in heaven, my Edward's breast
  This deed of mercy knew,
That gives my tortur'd bosom rest,
  He sure would bless thee too!

Oh tell me where my lover fell!
  The fatal scene recall,
His last, dear accents, stranger, tell,
  Oh haste and tell me all!

Say, if he gave to love the sigh,
  That set his spirit free;
Say, did he raise his closing eye,
  As if it sought for me."

"Ask not, her father cry'd, to know
  What known were added pain;
Nor think, my child, the tale of woe
  Thy softness can sustain."

"Tho' every joy with Edward fled,
  When Edward's friend is near,
It sooths my breaking heart, she said,
  To tell those joys were dear.

The western ocean roll'd in vain

Its parting waves between,
My Edward brav'd the dang'rous main,
  And bless'd our native scene.

Soft Isis heard his artless tale,
  Ah, stream for ever dear!
Whose waters, as they pass'd the vale,
  Receiv'd a lover's tear.

How could a heart, that virtue lov'd,
  (And sure that heart is mine)
Lamented youth! behold unmov'd,
  The virtues that were thine?

Calm, as the surface of the lake,
  When all the winds are still,
Mild, as the beams of morning break,
  When first they light the hill;

So calm was his unruffled soul,
  Where no rude passion strove;
So mild his soothing accents stole,
  Upon the ear of love.

Where are the dear illusions fled
  Which sooth'd my former hours?
Where is the path that fancy spread,
  Ah, vainly spread with flowers!

I heard the battle's fearful sounds,
  They seem'd my lover's knell--
I heard, that pierc'd with ghastly wounds,
  My vent'rous lover fell!--

My sorrows shall with life endure,
  For he I lov'd is gone;
But something tells my heart, that sure
  My life will not be long."--

"My panting soul can bear no more,
  The youth, impatient cried,
'Tis Edward bids thy griefs be o'er,
  My love! my destin'd bride!

The life which heav'n preserv'd, how blest,
  How fondly priz'd by me,
Since dear to my Amelia's breast,
  Since valued still by thee!

My father saw my constant pain,
  When thee I left behind,
Nor longer will his power restrain,
  The ties my soul would bind.

And soon thy honor'd sire shall cease
  The captive's lot to bear,
And we, my love, will soothe to peace
  His griefs, with filial care.

Then come for ever to my soul!
  Amelia come, and prove!
How calm our blissful years will roll,
  Along a life of love!--

SONNET,
To MRS. BATES.

Oh, thou whose melody the heart obeys,
Thou who can'st all its subject passions move,
Whose notes to heav'n the list'ning soul can raise,
Can thrill with pity, or can melt with love!
Happy! whom nature lent this native charm;
Whose melting tones can shed with magic power,
A sweeter pleasure o'er the social hour,
The breast to softness sooth, to virtue warm--But
yet more happy! that thy life as clear
From discord, as thy perfect cadence flows;
That tun'd to sympathy, thy faithful tear,
In mild accordance falls for others woes;
That all the tender, pure affections bind
In chains of harmony, thy willing mind!

SONNET
To TWILIGHT.

Meek Twilight! soften the declining day,
  And bring the hour my pensive spirit loves;
When, o'er the mountain flow descends the ray
  That gives to silence the deserted groves.
Ah, let the happy court the morning still,
  When, in her blooming loveliness array'd,
She bids fresh beauty light the vale, or hill,
  And rapture warble in the vocal shade.
Sweet is the odour of the morning's flower,
  And rich in melody her accents rise;
Yet dearer to my soul the shadowy hour,
  At which her blossoms close, her music dies--
For then, while languid nature droops her head,
She wakes the tear 'tis luxury to shed.

TO
SENSIBILITY.

In *Sensibility's* lov'd praise
  I tune my trembling reed;
And seek to deck her shrine with bays,
  On which my heart must bleed!

No cold exemption from her pain
  I ever wish'd to know;
Cheer'd with her transport, I sustain
  Without complaint her woe.

Above whate'er content can give,
  Above the charm of ease,
The restless hopes, and fears that live
  With her, have power to please.

Where but for her, were Friendship's power
  To heal the wounded heart,
To shorten sorrow's ling'ring hour,
  And bid its gloom depart?

'Tis she that lights the melting eye
  With looks to anguish dear;
She knows the price of ev'ry sigh,

The value of a tear.

She prompts the tender marks of love
  Which words can scarce express;
The heart alone their force can prove,
  And feel how much they bless.

Of every finer bliss the source!
  'Tis she on love bestows
The softer grace, the boundless force
  Confiding passion knows;

When to another, the fond breast
  Each thought for ever gives;
When on another, leans for rest.
  And in another lives!

Quick, as the trembling metal flies,
  When heat or cold impels,
Her anxious heart to joy can rise,
  Or sink where anguish dwells!

Yet tho' her soul must griefs sustain
  Which she alone, can know;
And feel that keener sense of pain
  Which sharpens every woe;

Tho' she the mourner's grief to calm,
  Still shares each pang they feel,
And, like the tree distilling balm,
  Bleeds, others wounds to heal;

While she, whose bosom fondly true,

Has never wish'd to range;
One alter'd look will trembling view,
  And scarce can bear the change;

Tho' she, if death the bands should tear,
  She vainly thought secure;
Thro' life must languish in despair
  That never hopes a cure;

Tho' wounded by some vulgar mind,
  Unconscious of the deed,
Who never seeks those wounds to bind
  But wonders why they bleed;--

She oft will heave a secret sigh,
  Will shed a lonely tear,
O'er feelings nature wrought so high,
  And gave on terms so dear;

Yet who would hard INDIFFERENCE choose,
  Whose breast no tears can steep?
Who, for her apathy, would lose
  The sacred power to weep?

Tho' in a thousand objects, pain,
  And pleasure tremble nigh,
Those objects strive to reach, in vain,
  The circle of her eye.

Cold, as the fabled god appears
  To the poor suppliant's grief,
Who bathes the marble form in tears,
  And vainly hopes relief.

Ah *Greville!* why the gifts refuse
  To souls like thine allied?
No more thy nature seem to lose
  No more thy softness hide.

No more invoke the playful sprite
  To chill, with magic spell,
The tender feelings of delight,
  And anguish sung so well;

That envied ease thy heart would prove
  Were sure too dearly bought
With friendship, sympathy, and love,
  And every finer thought.

A SONG.

I.

No riches from his scanty store
  My lover could impart;
He gave a boon I valued more--
  He gave me all his heart!

II.

His soul sincere, his gen'rous worth,
  Might well this bosom move;
And when I ask'd for bliss on earth,
  I only meant his love.

III.

But now for me, in search of gain
  From shore to shore he flies:
Why wander riches to obtain,
  When love is all I prize?

IV.

The frugal meal, the lowly cot
  If blest my love with thee!
That simple fare, that humble lot,
  Were more than wealth to me.

V.

While he the dang'rous ocean braves,
  My tears but vainly flow:
Is pity in the faithless waves
  To which I pour my woe?

VI.

The night is dark, the waters deep,
  Yet soft the billows roll;
Alas! at every breeze I weep--
  The storm is in my soul.

AN ODE ON THE PEACE.

I.

As wand'ring late on Albion's shore
   That chains the rude tempestuous deep,
 I heard the hollow surges roar
   And vainly beat her guardian steep;
I heard the rising sounds of woe
   Loud on the storm's wild pinion flow;
And still they vibrate on the mournful lyre,
That tunes to grief its sympathetic wire.

II.

From shores the wide Atlantic laves,
   The spirit of the ocean bears
 In moans, along his western waves,
   Afflicted nature's hopeless cares:
 Enchanting scenes of young delight,
   How chang'd since first ye rose to sight;
Since first ye rose in infant glories drest
Fresh from the wave, and rear'd your ample breast.

III.

   Her crested serpents, discord throws
     O'er scenes which love with roses grac'd;
   The flow'ry chain his hands compose,
     She wildly scatters o'er the waste:
   Her glance his playful smile deforms,
   Her frantic voice awakes the storms,
From land to land, her torches spread their fires,
While love's pure flame in streams of blood expires.

IV.

   Now burns the savage soul of war,
     While terror flashes from his eyes,
   Lo! waving o'er his fiery car
     Aloft his bloody banner flies:
The battle wakes--with awful sound
   He thunders o'er the echoing ground,
He grasps his reeking blade, while streams of blood
Tinge the vast plain, and swell the purple flood.

V.

   But softer sounds of sorrow flow;
     On drooping wing the murm'ring gales
Have borne the deep complaints of woe
     That rose along the lonely vales--
Those breezes waft the orphan's cries,
They tremble to parental sighs,

And drink a tear for keener anguish shed,
The tear of faithful love when hope is fled.

VI.

The object of her anxious fear
  Lies pale on earth, expiring, cold,
Ere, wing'd by happy love, one year
  Too rapid in its course, has roll'd;
In vain the dying hand she grasps,
  Hangs on the quiv'ring lip, and clasps
The fainting form, that slowly sinks in death,
To catch the parting glance, the fleeting breath.

VII.

Pale as the livid corse her cheek,
  Her tresses torn, her glances wild,--
How fearful was her frantic shriek!
  She wept--and then in horrors smil'd:
She gazes now with wild affright,
  Lo! bleeding phantoms rush in sight--
Hark! on yon mangled form the mourner calls,
Then on the earth a senseless weight she falls.

VIII.

And see! o'er gentle Andre's tomb,
  The victim of his own despair,
  Who fell in life's exulting bloom,

Nor deem'd that life deserv'd a care;
  O'er the cold earth his relicks prest,
  Lo! Britain's drooping legions rest;
For him the swords they sternly grasp, appear
Dim with a sigh, and sullied with a tear.

IX.

While Seward sweeps her plaintive strings,
  While pensive round his sable shrine,
  A radiant zone she graceful flings,
    Where full emblaz'd his virtues shine;
  The mournful loves that tremble nigh
  Shall catch her warm melodious sigh;
The mournful loves shall drink the tears that flow
From Pity's hov'ring soul, dissolv'd in woe.

X.

And hark, in Albion's flow'ry vale
  A parent's deep complaint I hear!
  A sister calls the western gale
    To waft her soul-expressive tear;
'Tis Asgill claims that piercing sigh,
  That drop which dims the beauteous eye,
While on the rack of Doubt Affection proves
How strong the force which binds the ties she loves.

XI.

How oft in every dawning grace
   That blossom'd in his early hours,
Her soul some comfort lov'd to trace,
   And deck'd futurity in flowers!
But lo! in Fancy's troubled sight
The dear illusions sink in night;
She views the murder'd form--the quiv'ring breath,
The rising virtues chill'd in shades of death.

XII.

Cease, cease ye throbs of hopeless woe;
   He lives the future hours to bless,
He lives, the purest joy to know,
   Parental transports fond excess;
His sight a father's eye shall chear,
   A sister's drooping charms endear:--
The private pang was Albion's gen'rous care,
For him she breath'd a warm accepted prayer.

XIII.

And lo! a radiant stream of light
   Defending, gilds the murky cloud,
Where Desolation's gloomy night
   Retiring, folds her sable shroud;
It flashes o'er the bright'ning deep,
It softens Britain's frowning steep--

'Tis mild benignant Peace, enchanting form!
That gilds the black abyss, that lulls the storm.

XIV.

So thro' the dark, impending sky,
  Where clouds, and fallen vapours roll'd,
Their curling wreaths dissolving fly
  As the faint hues of light unfold--
The air with spreading azure streams,
The sun now darts his orient beams--
And now the mountains glow--the woods are bright--
While nature hails the season of delight.

XV.

Mild Peace! from Albion's fairest bowers
  Pure spirit! cull with snowy hands,
The buds that drink the morning showers,
  And bind the realms in flow'ry bands:
Thy smiles the angry passions chase,
Thy glance is pleasure's native grace;
Around thy form th' exulting virtues move,
And thy soft call awakes the strain of love.

XVI.

Bless, all ye powers! the patriot name
  That courts fair Peace, thy gentle stay;
Ah! gild with glory's light, his fame,

And glad his life with pleasure's ray!
While, like th' affrighted dove, thy form
  Still shrinks, and fears some latent storm,
His cares shall sooth thy panting soul to rest,
And spread thy vernal couch on Albion's breast.

XVII.

Ye, who have mourn'd the parting hour,
  Which love in darker horrors drew,
Ye, who have vainly tried to pour
  With falt'ring voice the last adieu!
  When the pale cheek, the bursting sigh,
  The soul that hov'ring in the eye,
Express'd the pains it felt, the pains it fear'd--
Ah! paint the youth's return, by grief endear'd.

XVIII.

Yon hoary form, with aspect mild,
  Deserted kneels by anguish prest,
And seeks from Heav'n his long-lost child,
  To smooth the path that leads to rest!--
  He comes!--to close the sinking eye,
  To catch the faint, expiring sigh;
A moment's transport stays the fleeting breath,
And sooths the soul on the pale verge of death.

XIX.

No more the sanguine wreath shall twine
   On the lost hero's early tomb,
But hung around thy simple shrine
   Fair Peace! shall milder glories bloom.
Lo! commerce lifts her drooping head
   Triumphal, Thames! from thy deep bed;
And bears to Albion, on her sail sublime,
The riches Nature gives each happier clime.

XX.

She fearless prints the polar snows,
   Mid' horrors that reject the day;
Along the burning line she glows,
   Nor shrinks beneath the torrid ray:
She opens India's glitt'ring mine,
   Where streams of light reflected shine;
Wafts the bright gems to Britain's temp'rate vale,
And breathes her odours on the northern gale.

XXI.

While from the far-divided shore
   Where liberty unconquer'd roves,
Her ardent glance shall oft' explore
   The parent isle her spirit loves;
Shall spread upon the western main
   --Harmonious concord's golden chain,

While stern on Gallia's ever hostile strand
From Albion's cliff she pours her daring band.

XXII.

  Yet hide the sabre's hideous glare
    Whose edge is bath'd in streams of blood,
  The lance that quivers high in air,
    And falling drinks a purple flood;
For Britain! fear shall seize thy foes,
  While freedom in thy senate glows,
While peace shall smile upon thy cultur'd plain,
With grace and beauty her attendant train.

XXIII.

  Enchanting visions sooth my sight--
    The finer arts no more oppress'd,
  Benignant source of pure delight!
    On her soft bosom love to rest.
  While each discordant sound expires,
  Strike harmony! strike all thy wires;
The fine vibrations of the spirit move
And touch the springs of rapture and of love.

XXIV.

  Bright painting's living forms shall rise;
    And wrapt in Ugolino's woe[A],
  Shall Reynolds wake unbidden sighs;

And Romney's graceful pencil flow,
  That Nature's look benign pourtrays[B],
  When to her infant Shakspeare's gaze
The partial nymph "unveil'd her awful face,"
And bade his "colours clear" her features trace.

[A] "Ugolino's woe"--a celebrated picture by Sir JOSHUA REYNOLDS, taken
    from DANTE.
[B] "Nature's look benign pourtrays"--a subject Mr. ROMNEY has taken
    from GRAY'S Progress of Poesy.

XXV.

And poesy! thy deep-ton'd shell
  The heart shall sooth, the spirit fire,
And all the passion sink, or swell,
  In true accordance to the lyre.
Oh! ever wake its heav'nly sound,
Oh! call thy lovely visions round;
Strew the soft path of peace with fancy's flowers,
With raptures bless the soul that feels thy powers.

XXVI.

While Hayley wakes thy magic string,
  His shades shall no rude sound profane,
But stillness on her folded wing,
  Enamour'd catch his soothing strain:
Tho' genius breathe its purest flame
--Around his lyre's enchanting frame;
Tho' music there in every period roll,

More warm his friendship, and more pure his soul.

XXVII.

  While taste refines a polish'd age,
    While her own ***Hurd*** shall bid us trace
  The lustre of the finish'd page
    Where symmetry sheds perfect grace;
  With sober and collected ray
  To fancy, judgment shall display
The faultless model, where accomplish'd art
From nature draws a charm that leads the heart.

XXVIII.

  Th' historic Muse illumes the maze
    For ages veil'd in gloomy night,
  Where empire with meridian blaze
    Once trod ambition's giddy height:
  Tho' headlong from the dang'rous steep
  Its pageants roll'd with wasteful sweep,
Her tablet still records the deeds of fame
And wakes the patriot's, and the hero's flame.

XXIX.

  While meek philosophy explores
    Creation's vast stupendous round;
  Sublime her piercing vision soars,
    And bursts the system's distant bound.

Lo! mid' the dark deep void of space
A rushing world[A] her eye can trace!--
It moves majestic in its ample sphere,
Sheds its long light, and rolls its ling'ring year.

[A] Alluding to Mr. Herschel's wonderful discoveries, and particularly
    to his discovery of a new planet called the Georgium Sidus.

XXX.

Ah! still diffuse thy genial ray,
   Fair Science, on my Albion's plain!
And still thy grateful homage pay
   Where Montagu has rear'd her fane;
Where eloquence and wit entwine
Their attic wreath around her shrine;
And still, while Learning shall unfold her store,
With their bright signet stamp the classic ore.

XXXI.

Enlight'ning Peace! for thine the hours
   That wisdom decks in moral grace,
And thine invention's fairy powers,
   The charm improv'd of nature's face;
Propitious come! in silence laid
Beneath thy olive's grateful shade,
Pour the mild bliss that sooths the tuneful mind,
And in thy zone the hostile spirit bind.

XXXII.

While Albion on her parent deep
  Shall rest, may glory light her shore,
May honour there his vigils keep
  Till time shall wing its course no more;
Till angels wrap the spheres in fire,
  Till earth and yon fair orbs expire,
While chaos mounted on the wasting flame,
Shall spread eternal shade o'er nature's frame.

EDWIN AND ELTRUDA,

A LEGENDARY TALE.

  Mark it, Cesario, it is old and plain;
  The spinsters and the knitters in the sun,
  And the free maids, that weave their thread with bones
  Do use to chant it. It is silly, sooth,
  And dallies with the innocence of love,
  Like the old age.
SHAKSPEARE'S TWELFTH NIGHT.

EDWIN AND ELTRUDA
A LEGENDARY TALE.

Where the pure Derwent's waters glide
  Along their mossy bed,
Close by the river's verdant side,
  A castle rear'd its head.

The ancient pile by time is raz'd,
  Where Gothic trophies frown'd;
Where once the gilded armour blaz'd,
  And banners wav'd around.

There liv'd a chief, well known to fame,
  A bold advent'rous knight;
Renown'd for victory; his name
  In glory's annals bright.

What time in martial pomp he led
  His gallant, chosen train;
The foe, who oft had conquer'd, fled,
  Indignant fled, the plain.

Yet milder virtues he possest,
  And gentler passions felt;

For in his calm and yielding breast
  The soft affections dwelt.

No rugged toils the heart could steel,
  By nature form'd to prove
Whate'er the tender mind can feel,
  In friendship, or in love.

He lost the partner of his breast,
  Who sooth'd each rising care;
And ever charm'd the pains to rest
  She ever lov'd to share.

From solitude he hop'd relief.
  And this lone mansion sought,
To cherish there his faithful grief,
  To nurse the tender thought.

There, to his bosom fondly dear,
  An infant daughter smil'd,
And oft the mourner's falling tear
  Bedew'd his Emma's child.

The tear, as o'er the babe he hung,
  Would tremble in his eye;
While blessings, falt'ring on his tongue,
  Were breath'd but in a sigh.

Tho' time could never heal the wound,
  It sooth'd the hopeless pain;
And in his child he thought he found
  His Emma liv'd again.

Soft, as the dews of morn arise,
  And on the pale flower gleam;
So soft Eltruda's melting eyes
  With love and pity beam.

As drest in charms, the lonely flower
  Smiles in the desert vale;
With beauty gilds the morning hour,
  And scents the evening gale;

So liv'd in solitude, unseen,
  This lovely, peerless maid;
So grac'd the wild, sequester'd scene,
  And blossom'd in the shade.

Yet love could pierce the lone recess,
  For there he likes to dwell;
To leave the noisy crowd, and bless
  With happiness the cell.

To wing his sure resistless dart,
  Where all its force is known;
And rule the undivided heart
  Despotic, and alone.

Young Edwin charm'd her gentle breast,
  Tho' scanty all his store;
No hoarded treasures he possest,
  Yet he could boast of more.

For he could boast the lib'ral heart;
  And honour, sense, and truth,
Unwarp'd by vanity or art,

Adorn'd the gen'rous youth.

The maxims of a servile age,
  The mean, the selfish care,
The sordid views, that now engage
  The mercenary pair;

Whom riches can unite, or part,
  To them were still unknown;
For then the sympathetic heart
  Was join'd by love alone.

They little knew, that wealth had power
  To make the constant rove;
They little knew the weighty dower
  Could add one bliss to love.

Her virtues every charm improv'd,
  Or made those charms more dear;
For surely virtue to be lov'd
  Has only to appear.

Domestic bliss, unvex'd by strife,
  Beguil'd the circling hours;
She, who on every path of life
  Can shed perennial flowers.

Eltruda, o'er the distant mead,
  Would haste, at closing day,
And to the bleating mother lead
  The lamb, that chanc'd to stray.

For the bruis'd insect on the waste,
  A sigh would heave her breast;
And oft her careful hand replac'd
  The linnet's falling nest.

To her, sensations calm as these
  Could sweet delight impart;
These simple pleasures most can please
  The uncorrupted heart.

Full oft with eager step she flies
  To cheer the roofless cot,
Where the lone widow breathes her sighs,
  And wails her desp'rate lot.

Their weeping mother's trembling knees,
  Her lisping infants clasp;
Their meek, imploring look she sees,
  She feels their tender grasp.

Wild throbs her aching bosom swell--
  They mark the bursting sigh,
(Nature has form'd the soul to feel)
  They weep, unknowing why.

Her hands the lib'ral boon impart,
  And much her tear avails
To raise the mourner's drooping heart,
  Where feeble utterance fails.

On the pale cheek, where hung the tear
  Of agonizing woe,
She bids the cheerful bloom appear,

The tear of rapture flow.

Thus on soft wing the moments flew,
  (Tho' love implor'd their stay)
While some new virtue rose to view,
  And mark'd each fleeting day.

The youthful poet's soothing dream
  Of golden ages past;
The muse's fond, ideal theme,
  Was realiz'd at last.

But vainly here we hope, that bliss
  Unchanging will endure;
Ah, in a world so vain as this,
  What heart can rest secure!

For now arose the fatal day
  For civil discord fam'd;
When **York**, from **Lancaster's** proud sway,
  The regal sceptre claim'd.

Each moment now the horrors brought
  Of desolating rage;
The fam'd atchievements now were wrought,
  That swell th' historic page.

The good old Albert pants, again
  To dare the hostile field,
The cause of Henry to maintain,
  For him, the launce to wield.

But oh, a thousand gen'rous ties,
  That bind the hero's soul;
A thousand tender claims arise,
  And Edwin's breast controul.

Tho' passion pleads in Henry's cause,
  And Edwin's heart would sway;
Yet honour's stern, imperious laws,
  The brave will still obey.

Oppress'd with many an anxious care,
  Full oft Eltruda sigh'd;
Complaining that relentless war
  Should those she lov'd--divide.

At length the parting morn arose,
  In gloomy vapours drest;
The pensive maiden's sorrow flows,
  And terror heaves her breast.

A thousand pangs the father feels,
  A thousand rising fears,
While clinging at his feet she kneels,
  And bathes them with her tears.

A pitying tear bedew'd his cheek,--
  From his lov'd child he flew;
O'erwhelm'd; the father could not speak,
  He could not say--"adieu!"

Arm'd for the field, her lover
  He saw her pallid look,
And trembling seize her drooping frame,

While fault'ring, thus he spoke:

"This cruel tenderness but wounds
  "The heart it means to bless;
"Those falling tears, those mournful sounds
  "Increase the vain distress."--

"If fate, she answer'd, has decreed
  "That on the hostile plain,
"My Edwin's faithful heart must bleed,
  "And swell the heap of slain;

"Trust me, my love, I'll not complain,
  "I'll shed no fruitless tear;
"Not one weak drop my cheek shall stain,
  "Or tell what passes here!

"Oh, let thy fate of others claim
  "A tear, a mournful sigh;
"I'll only murmur thy dear name--
  Call on my love--and die!"

But ah! how vain for words to tell
  The pang their bosoms prov'd;
They only will conceive it well,
  They only, who have lov'd.

The timid muse forbears to say
  What laurels Edwin gain'd;
How Albert long renown'd, that day
  His ancient fame maintain'd.

The bard, who feels congenial fire,
  May sing of martial strife;
And with heroic sounds, inspire
  The gen'rous scorn of life;

But ill the theme would suit her reed,
  Who, wand'ring thro' the grove,
Forgets the conq'ring hero's meed,
  And gives a tear to love.

Tho' long the closing day was fled,
  The fight they still maintain;
While night a deeper horror shed
  Along the darken'd plain.

To Albert's breast an arrow flew,
  He felt a mortal wound;
The drops that warm'd his heart, bedew
  The cold, and flinty ground.

The foe, who aim'd the fatal dart,
  Now heard his dying sighs;
Compassion touch'd his yielding heart,
  To Albert's aid he flies.

While round the chief his arms he cast,
  While oft he deeply sigh'd,
And seem'd, as if he mourn'd the past,
  Old Albert faintly cried;

"Tho' nature heaves these parting groans,
  "Without complaint I die;
"Yet one dear care my heart still owns,

"Still feels one tender tie,

"For York, a warriour known to fame,
  "Uplifts the hostile spear;
"Edwin the blooming hero's name,
  "To Albert's bosom dear.

"Oh, tell him my expiring sigh,
  "Say my last words implor'd
"To my despairing child to fly,
  "To her he once ador'd"--

He spoke! but oh, what mournful strain,
  Whose force the soul can melt,
What moving numbers shall explain
  The pang that Edwin felt?

The pang that Edwin now reveal'd--
  For he the warriour prest,
(Whom the dark shades of night conceal'd)
  Close to his throbbing breast.

"Fly, fly he cried, my touch profane--
  "Oh, how the rest impart?
"Rever'd old man!--could Edwin stain
  "With Albert's blood the dart!"

His languid eyes he meekly rais'd,
  Which seem'd for ever clos'd;
On the pale youth with pity gaz'd,
  And then in death repos'd.

"I'll go, the hapless Edwin said,
   "And breathe a last adieu!
"And with the drops despair will shed,
   "My mournful love bedew.

"I'll go to her for ever dear,
   "To catch her melting sigh,
"To wipe from her pale cheek the tear,
   "And at her feet to die."--

And as to her for ever dear
   The frantic mourner flew,
To wipe from her pale cheek the tear,
   And breathe a last adieu;

Appall'd his troubled fancy sees
   Eltruda's anguish flow;
And hears in every passing breeze,
   The plaintive sound of woe.

Meanwhile the anxious maid, whose tears
   In vain would heav'n implore;
Of Albert's fate despairing hears,
   But yet had heard no more.

She saw her much-lov'd Edwin near,
   She saw, and deeply sigh'd;
Her cheek was bath'd in many a tear;
   At length she faintly cried;

"Unceasing grief this heart must prove,
   "Its dearest ties are broke;--
"Oh, say, what ruthless arm, my love,

"Could aim the fatal stroke?

"Could not thy hand, my Edwin, thine,
  "Have warded off the blow?
"For oh, he was not only mine,
  "He was *thy* father too!"

No more the youth could pangs endure
  His lips could never tell;
From death he vainly hop'd a cure,
  As cold, on earth he fell.

She flew, she gave her sorrows vent,
  A thousand tears she pour'd;
Her mournful voice, her moving plaint,
  The youth to life restor'd.

"Why does thy bosom throb with pain
  "She cried, my Edwin, speak;
"Or sure, unable to sustain
  "This grief, my heart will break.

"Yes, it will break--he fault'ring cried,
  "For me will life resign--
"Then trembling know thy father died--
  "And know the guilt was mine!"

"It is enough," with short, quick breath,
  Exclaim'd the fainting maid;
She spoke no more, but seem'd from death
  To look for instant aid.

In plaintive accents, Edwin cries,
  "And have I murder'd thee?
"To other worlds thy spirit flies,
  "And mine this stroke shall free."

His hand the lifted weapon grasp'd,
  The steel he firmly prest:
When wildly she arose, and clasp'd
  Her lover to her breast.

"Methought, she cried with panting breath,
  "My Edwin talk'd of peace;
"I knew 'twas only found in death,
  "And fear'd that sad release.

"I clasp him still! 'twas but a dream--
  "Help yon wide wound to close,
"From which a father's spirits stream,
  "A father's life-blood flows.

"But see, from thee he shrinks, nor would
  "Be blasted by thy touch;--
"Ah, tho' my Edwin spilt thy blood,
  "Yet once he lov'd thee much.

"My father, yet in pity stay!--
  "I see his white beard wave;
"A spirit beckons him away,
  "And points to yonder grave.

"Alas, my love, I trembling hear
  "A father's last adieu;
"I see, I see, the falling tear

"His wrinkled cheek bedew.

"He's gone, and here his ashes sleep--
  "I do not heave a sigh,
"His child a father does not weep--
  "For, ah, my brain is dry!

"But come, together let us rove,
  "At the pale hour of night;
"When the moon wand'ring thro' the grove,
  "Shall pour her faintest light.

"We'll gather from the rosy bow'r
  "The fairest wreaths that bloom:
"We'll cull, my love, each op'ning flower,
  "To deck his hallow'd tomb.

"We'll thither, from the distant dale,
  "A weeping willow bear;
"And plant a lily of the vale,
  "A drooping lily there.

"We'll shun the face of glaring day,
  "Eternal silence keep;
"Thro' the dark wood together stray,
  "And only live to weep.

"But hark, 'tis come--the fatal time
  "When, Edwin, we must part;
"Some angel tells me 'tis a crime
  "To hold thee to my heart.

"My father's spirit hovers near--
   "Alas, he comes to chide;
"Is there no means, my Edwin dear,
   "The fatal deed to hide?

"Yet, Edwin, if th' offence be thine,
   "Too soon I can forgive;
"But, oh, the guilt would all be mine,
   "Could I endure to live.

"Farewel, my love, for, oh, I faint,
   "Of pale despair I die;
"And see, that hoary, murder'd saint
   "Descends from yon blue sky.

"Poor, weak old man! he comes my love,
   "To lead to heav'n the way;
"He knows not heaven will joyless prove,
   "If Edwin here must stay!"--

"Oh, who can bear this pang!" he cry'd,
   Then to his bosom prest
The dying maid, who piteous sigh'd,
   And sunk to endless rest.

He saw her eyes for ever close,
   He heard her latest sigh,
And yet no tear of anguish flows
   From his distracted eye.

He feels within his shiv'ring veins,
   A mortal chillness rise;
Her pallid corse he feebly strains--

And on her bosom dies.

* * * * *

No longer may their hapless lot
  The mournful muse engage;
She wipes away the tears, that blot
  The melancholy page.

For heav'n in love, dissolves the ties
  That chain the spirit here;
And distant far for ever flies
  The blessing held most dear;

To bid the suff'ring soul aspire
  A higher bliss to prove;
To wake the pure, refin'd desire,
  The hope that rests above!--

A HYMN.

While thee I seek, protecting Power!
　Be my vain wishes still'd;
And may this consecrated hour
　With better hopes be fill'd.

Thy love the powers of thought bestow'd,
　To thee my thoughts would soar;
Thy mercy o'er my life has flow'd--
　That mercy I adore.

In each event of life, how clear,
　Thy ruling hand I see;
Each blessing to my soul more dear,
　Because conferr'd by thee.

In every joy that crowns my days,
　In every pain I bear,
My heart shall find delight in praise,
　Or seek relief in prayer.

When gladness wings my favour'd hour,
　Thy love my thoughts shall fill:
Resign'd, when storms of sorrow lower,

My soul shall meet thy will.

My lifted eye without a tear
  The lowring storm shall see;
My stedfast heart shall know no fear--
  That heart will rest on Thee!

PARAPHRASES FROM SCRIPTURE.

The day is thine, the night also is thine; thou hast prepared the light and the sun.

Thou hast set all the borders of the earth; thou hast made summer and winter.

PSALM lxxiv. , .

My God! all nature owns thy sway,
Thou giv'st the night, and thou the day!
When all thy lov'd creation wakes,
When morning, rich in lustre breaks,
And bathes in dew the op'ning flower,
To thee we owe her fragrant hour;
And when she pours her choral song,
Her melodies to thee belong!

Or when, in paler tints array'd,
The evening slowly spreads her shade;
That soothing shade, that grateful gloom,
Can more than day's enliv'ning bloom
Still every fond, and vain desire,
And calmer, purer, thoughts inspire;

From earth the pensive spirit free,
And lead the soften'd heart to Thee.

  In every scene thy hands have drest,
In every form by thee imprest,
Upon the mountain's awful head,
Or where the shelt'ring woods are spread;
In every note that swells the gale,
Or tuneful stream that cheers the vale,
The cavern's depth, or echoing grove,
A voice is heard of praise, and love.

As o'er thy work the seasons roll,
And sooth with change of bliss, the soul,
Oh never may their smiling train
Pass o'er the human scene in vain!
But oft as on the charm we gaze,
Attune the wond'ring soul to praise;
And be the joys that most we prize,
The joys that from thy favour rise!

Can a woman forget her sucking child, that she should
not have compassion on the son of her womb? Yea,
they may forget, yet will I not forget thee.

ISAIAH xlix. .

Heaven speaks! Oh Nature listen and rejoice!
Oh spread from pole to pole this gracious voice!
"Say every breast of human frame, that proves
"The boundless force with which a parent loves;
"Say, can a mother from her yearning heart
"Bid the soft image of her child depart?
"She! whom strong instinct arms with strength to bear
"All forms of ill, to shield that dearest care;
"She! who with anguish stung, with madness wild,
"Will rush on death to save her threaten'd child;
"All selfish feelings banish'd from her breast,
"Her life one aim to make another's blest.
"When her vex'd infant to her bosom clings,
"When round her neck his eager arms he flings;
"Breathes to her list'ning soul his melting sigh,
"And lifts suffus'd with tears his asking eye!
"Will she for all ambition can attain,
"The charms of pleasure, or the lures of gain,
"Betray strong Nature's feelings, will she prove
"Cold to the claims of duty, and of love?
"But should the mother from her yearning heart
"Bid the soft image of her child depart;
"When the vex'd infant to her bosom clings
"When round her neck his eager arms he flings;

"Should she unpitying hear his melting sigh,
"And view unmov'd the tear that fills his eye;
"Should she for all ambition can attain,
"The charms of pleasure, or the lures of gain,
"Betray strong Nature's feelings--should she prove
"Cold to the claims of duty, and of love!
"Yet never will the God, whose word gave birth
"To yon illumin'd orbs, and this fair earth;
"Who thro' the boundless depths of trackless space
"Bade new-wak'd beauty spread each perfect grace;
"Yet when he form'd the vast stupendous whole,
"Shed his best bounties on the human soul;
"Which reason's light illumes, which friendship warms,
"Which pity softens, and which virtue charms;
"Which feels the pure affections gen'rous glow,
"Shares others joy, and bleeds for others woe--
"Oh never will the gen'ral Father prove
"Of man forgetful, man the child of love!"
When all those planets in their ample spheres
Have wing'd their course, and roll'd their destin'd years;
When the vast sun shall veil his golden light
Deep in the gloom of everlasting night;
When wild, destructive flames shall wrap the skies,
When Chaos triumphs, and when Nature dies;
Man shall alone the wreck of worlds survive,
Midst falling spheres, immortal man shall live!
The voice which bade the last dread thunders roll,
Shall whisper to the good, and cheer their soul.
God shall himself his favour'd creature guide
Where living waters pour their blissful tide,
Where the enlarg'd, exulting, wond'ring mind
Shall soar, from weakness and from guilt refin'd;
Where perfect knowledge, bright with cloudless rays,

Shall gild eternity's unmeasur'd days;
Where friendship, unembitter'd by distrust,
Shall in immortal bands unite the just;
Devotion rais'd to rapture breathe her strain,
And love in his eternal triumph reign!

Whatsoever ye would that men should do to you, do ye even so to them.

MATT. vii. .

Precept divine! to earth in mercy given,
O sacred rule of action, worthy heaven!
Whose pitying love ordain'd the bless'd command
To bind our nature in a firmer band;
Enforce each human suff'rer's strong appeal,
And teach the selfish breast what others feel;
Wert thou the guide of life, mankind might know
A soft exemption from the worst of woe;
No more the powerful would the weak oppress,
But tyrants learn the luxury to bless;
No more would slav'ry bind a hopeless train,
Of human victims, in her galling chain;
Mercy the hard, the cruel heart would move
To soften mis'ry by the deeds of Jove;
And av'rice from his hoarded treasures give
Unask'd, the liberal boon, that want might live!
The impious tongue of falshood then would cease
To blast, with dark suggestions, virtue's peace;
No more would spleen, or passion banish rest
And plant a pang in fond affection's breast;
By one harsh word, one alter'd look, destroy
Her peace, and wither every op'ning joy;
Scarce can her tongue the captious wrong explain,
The slight offence which gives so deep a pain!

Th' affected ease that slights her starting tear,
The words whose coldness kills from lips so dear;
The hand she loves, alone can point the dart,
Whose hidden sting could wound no other heart--
These, of all pains the sharpest we endure,
The breast which now inflicts, would spring to cure.--
No more deserted genius then, would fly
To breathe in solitude his hopeless sigh;
No more would Fortune's partial smile debase
The spirit, rich in intellectual grace;
Who views unmov'd from scenes where pleasures bloom,
The flame of genius sunk in mis'ry's gloom;
The soul heav'n form'd to soar, by want deprest,
Nor heeds the wrongs that pierce a kindred breast.--
Thou righteous Law! whose clear and useful light
Sheds on the mind a ray divinely bright;
Condensing in one rule whate'er the sage
Has proudly taught, in many a labour'd page;
Bid every heart thy hallow'd voice revere,
To justice sacred, and to nature dear!

AN EPISTLE TO DR. MOORE.

Whether dispensing hope, and ease
To the pale victim of disease,
Or in the social crowd you sit,
And charm the group with sense and wit,
Moore's partial ear will not disdain
Attention to my artless strain.

AN EPISTLE TO DR. MOORE,

AUTHOR OF A VIEW OF SOCIETY AND MANNERS IN FRANCE,
SWITZERLAND, AND GERMANY.

I mean no giddy heights to climb,
And vainly toil to be sublime;
While every line with labour wrought,
Is swell'd with tropes for want of thought:
Nor shall I call the Muse to shed
Castalian drops upon my head;
Or send me from Parnassian bowers
A chaplet wove of fancy's flowers.
At present all such aid I slight--
My heart instructs me how to write.

  That softer glide my hours along,
That still my griefs are sooth'd by song,
That still my careless numbers flow
To your successful skill I owe;
You, who when sickness o'er me hung,
And languor had my lyre unstrung,
With treasures of the healing art,
With friendship's ardor at your heart,
From sickness snatch'd her early prey
And bade fair health--the goddess gay,

With sprightly air, and winning grace,
With laughing eye, and rosy face,
Accustom'd when you call to hear,
On her light pinion hasten near,
And swift restore with influence kind,
My weaken'd frame, my drooping mind.

  With like benignity, and zeal,
The mental malady to heal,
To stop the fruitless, hopeless tear,
The life you lengthen'd, render dear,
To charm by fancy's powerful vein,
"The written troubles of the brain,"
From gayer scenes, compassion led
Your frequent footsteps to my shed:
And knowing that the Muses' art
Has power to ease an aching heart,
You sooth'd that heart with partial praise,
And I before too fond of lays,
While others pant for solid gain,
Grasp at a laurel sprig--in vain--
You could not chill with frown severe
The madness to my soul so dear;
For when Apollo came to store
Your mind with salutary lore,
The god I ween, was pleas'd to dart
A ray from Pindus on your heart;
Your willing bosom caught the fire,
And still is partial to the lyre.

  But now from you at distance plac'd
Where *Epping* spreads a woody waste;
Tho' unrestrain'd my fancy flies,

And views in air her fabrics rise,
And paints with brighter bloom the flowers,
Bids Dryads people all the bowers,
And Echoes speak from every hill,
And Naiads pour each little rill,
And bands of Sylphs with pride unfold
Their azure plumage mix'd with gold,
My heart remembers with a sigh
That you are now no longer nigh.
The magic scenes no more engage,
I quit them for your various page;
Where, with delight I traverse o'er
The foreign paths you trod before:
Ah not in vain those paths you trac'd,
With heart to feel, with powers to taste!

    Amid the ever-jocund train
Who sport upon the banks of Seine,
In your light Frenchman pleas'd I see
His nation's gay epitome;
Whose careless hours glide smooth along,
Who charms MISFORTUNE with a song.
She comes not as on Albion's plain,
With death, and madness in her train;
For here, her keenest sharpest dart
May raze, but cannot pierce the heart.
Yet he whose spirit light as air
Calls life a jest, and laughs at care,
Feels the strong force of pity's voice,
And bids afflicted love rejoice;
Love, such as fills the poet's page
Love, such as form'd the golden age--
FANCHON, thy grateful look I see--

I share thy joys--I weep with thee--
What eye has read without a tear
A tale to nature's heart so dear!

There, dress'd in each sublimer grace
Geneva's happy scene I trace;
Her lake, from whose broad bosom thrown
Rushes the loud impetuous Rhone,
And bears his waves with mazy sweep
In rapid torrents to the deep--
Oh for a Muse less weak of wing,
High on yon Alpine steeps to spring,
And tell in verse what they disclose
As well as you have told in prose;
How wrapt in snows and icy showers,
Eternal winter, horrid lowers
Upon the mountain's awful brow,
While purple summer blooms below;
How icy structures rear their forms
Pale products of ten thousand storms;
Where the full sun-beam powerless falls
On crystal arches, columns, walls,
Yet paints the proud fantastic height
With all the various hues of light.
Why is no poet call'd to birth
In such a favour'd spot of earth?
How high his vent'rous Muse might rise,
And proudly scorn to ask supplies
From the Parnassian hill, the fire
Of verse, **Mont Blanc** might well inspire.
O SWITZERLAND! how oft these eyes
Desire to view thy mountains rise;
How fancy loves thy steeps to climb,

So wild, so solemn, so sublime;
And o'er thy happy vales to roam,
Where freedom rears her humble home.
Ah, how unlike each social grace
Which binds in love thy manly race,
The HOLLANDERS phlegmatic ease
Too cold to love, too dull to please;
Who feel no sympathetic woe,
Nor sympathetic joy bestow,
But fancy words are only made
To serve the purposes of trade,
And when they neither buy, nor sell,
Think silence answers quite as well.

  Now in his happiest light is seen
VOLTAIRE, when evening chas'd his spleen,
And plac'd at supper with his friends,
The playful flash of wit descends--
Of names renown'd you clearly shew
The finer traits we wish to know--
To Prussia's martial clime I stray
And see how FREDERIC spends the day;
Behold him rise at dawning light
To form his troops for future fight;
Thro' the firm ranks his glances pierce,
Where discipline, with aspect fierce,
And unrelenting breast, is seen
Degrading man to a machine;
My female heart delights to turn
Where GREATNESS seems not quite so stern:
Mild on th' IMPERIAL BROW she glows,
And lives to soften human woes.

But lo! on ocean's stormy breast
I see majestic VENICE rest;
While round her spires the billows rave,
Inverted splendours gild the wave.
Fair liberty has rear'd with toil,
Her fabric on this marshy soil.
She fled those banks with scornful pride,
Where classic Po devolves her tide:
Yet here her unrelenting laws
Are deaf to nature's, freedom's cause.
Unjust! they seal'd FOSCARI'S doom,
An exile in his early bloom.
And he, who bore the rack unmov'd,
Divided far from those he lov'd,
From all the social hour can give,
From all that make it bliss to live,
These worst of ills refus'd to bear,
And died, the victim of despair.

　An eye of wonder let me raise,
While on imperial ROME I gaze.
But oh! no more in glory bright
She fills with awe th' astonish'd sight:
Her mould'ring fanes in ruin trac'd,
Lie scatter'd on *Campania's* waste.
Nor only these--alas! we find
The wreck involves the human mind:
The lords of earth now drag a chain
Beneath a pontiff's feeble reign;
The soil that gave a *Cato* birth
No longer yields heroic worth,
Whose image lives but on the bust,
Or consecrates the medal's rust:

Yet if no heart of modern frame
Glows with the antient hero's flame,
The dire *Arena's* horrid stage
Is banish'd from this milder age;
Those savage virtues too are fled
At which the human feelings bled.

While now at *Virgil's* tomb you bend,
O let me on your steps attend!
Kneel on the turf that blossoms round,
And kiss, with lips devout, the ground.
I feel how oft his magic powers
Shed pleasure on my lonely hours.
Tho' hid from me the classic tongue,
In which his heav'nly strain was sung,
In *Dryden's* tuneful lines, I pierce
The shaded beauties of his verse.

Bright be the rip'ning beam, that shines
Fair FLORENCE, on thy purple vines!
And ever pure the fanning gale
That pants in Arno's myrtle vale!
Here, when the barb'rous northern race,
Dire foes to every muse, and grace,
Had doom'd the banish'd arts to roam
The lovely wand'rers found a home;
And shed round *Leo's* triple crown
Unfading rays of bright renown.
Who e'er has felt his bosom glow
With knowledge, or the wish to know;
Has e'er from books with transport caught
The rich accession of a thought;
Perceiv'd with conscious pride, he feels

The sentiment which taste reveals;
Let all who joys like these possess,
Thy vale, enchanting FLORENCE bless--
O had the arts benignant light
No more reviv'd from Gothic night,
Earth had been one vast scene of strife,
Or one drear void had sadden'd life;
Lost had been all the sage has taught,
The painter's sketch, the poet's thought,
The force of sense, the charm of wit,
Nor ever had your page been writ;
That soothing page, which care beguiles,
And dresses truth in fancy's smiles:
For not with hostile step you prest
Each foreign soil, a thankless guest!
While travellers who want the skill
To mark the shapes of good and ill,
With vacant stare thro' Europe range,
And deem all bad, because 'tis strange;
Thro' varying modes of life, you trace
The finer trait, the latent grace,
And where thro' every vain disguise
You view the human follies rise,
The stroke of irony you dart
With force to mend, not wound the heart.
While intellectual objects share
Your mind's extensive view, you bear,
Quite free from spleen's incumb'ring load,
The little evils on the road--
So, while the path of life I tread,
A path to me with briers spread;
Let me its tangled mazes spy
Like you, with gay, good-humour'd eye;

Nor at those thorny tracts repine,
The treasure of your friendship, mine.

Grange Hill, Essex.

PART OF AN IRREGULAR FRAGMENT, FOUND IN A DARK PASSAGE OF THE TOWER.

ADVERTISEMENT.

The following Poem is formed on a very singular and sublime idea. A young gentleman, possessed of an uncommon genius for drawing, on visiting the Tower of London, passing one door of a singular construction, asked what apartment it led to, and expressed a desire to have it opened. The person who shewed the place shook his head, and answered, "Heaven knows what is within that door--it has been shut for ages."--This answer made small impression on the other hearers; but a very deep one on the imagination of this youth. Gracious Heaven! an apartment shut up for ages--and in the Tower!

> "Ye Towers of Julius! London's lasting shame,
> By many a foul and midnight murder fed."

Genius builds on a slight foundation, and rears beautiful structures on "the baseless fabric of a vision." The above transient hint dwelt on the young man's fancy, and conjured into his memory all the murders which history records to have been committed in the Tower; Henry the Sixth, the Duke of Clarence, the two young princes, sons of Edward the Fourth, Sir Thomas Overbury, &c. He supposes all their ghosts assembled in this unexplored apartment, and to these his fertile imagination has added several others. One of the spectres raises an immense pall of black velvet, and discovers the remains of a murdered royal family, whose story is lost in the lapse of time.--The gloomy wildness of these images struck my imagination so forcibly, that endeavouring to catch the fire of the youth's pencil, this Fragment was produced.

PART OF AN IRREGULAR FRAGMENT, FOUND IN A DARK PASSAGE OF THE TOWER.

I.

Rise, winds of night! relentless tempests rise!
  Rush from the troubled clouds, and o'er me roll;
In this chill pause a deeper horror lies,
  A wilder fear appals my shudd'ring soul.--
'Twas on this day[A], this hour accurst,
  That Nature starting from repose
Heard the dire shrieks of murder burst--
  From infant innocence they rose,
    And shook these solemn towers!--
I shudd'ring pass that fatal room
For ages wrapt in central gloom;--
I shudd'ring pass that iron door
Which Fate perchance unlocks no more;
Death, smear'd with blood, o'er the dark portal lowers.

[A] The anniversary of the murder of Edward the Fifth, and his brother
    Richard, Duke of York.

II.

How fearfully my step resounds
  Along these lonely bounds:--
Spare, savage blast! the taper's quiv'ring fires,
  Deep in these gath'ring shades its flame expires.
    Ye host of heaven! the door recedes--
    It mocks my grasp--what unseen hands
      Have burst its iron bands?
    No mortal force this gate unbarr'd
    Where danger lives, which terrors guard--
    Dread powers! its screaming hinges close
      On this dire scene of impious deeds--
    My feet are fix'd!--Dismay has bound
    My step on this polluted ground--
  But lo! the pitying moon, a line of light
  Athwart the horrid darkness dimly throws,
And from yon grated window chases night.--

III.

  Ye visions that before me roll,
  That freeze my blood, that shake my soul!
    Are ye the phantoms of a dream?
  Pale spectres! are ye what ye seem?
    They glide more near--
      Their forms unfold!
    Fix'd are their eyes, on me they bend--
      Their glaring look is cold!
  And hark!--I hear
Sounds that the throbbing pulse of life suspend.

IV.

"No wild illusion cheats thy sight
  "With shapes that only live in night--
"Mark the native glories spread
  "Around my bleeding brow!
"The crown of Albion wreath'd my head,
  "And Gallia's lilies[A] twin'd below--
"When my father shook his spear,
  "When his banner sought the skies,
"Her baffled host recoil'd with fear,
   "Nor turn'd their shrinking eyes:--
"Soon as the daring eagle springs
  "To bask in heav'n's empyreal light,
"The vultures ply their baleful wings,
  "A cloud of deep'ning colour marks their flight,
   "Staining the golden day:--
"But see! amid the rav'nous brood
  "A bird of fiercer aspect soar--
"The spirits of a rival race[B],
"Hang on the noxious blast, and trace,
  "With gloomy joy his destin'd prey;
"Inflame th' ambitious with that thirsts for blood,
"And plunge his talons deep in kindred gore.

[A] Henry the Sixth, crowned when an infant, at Paris.
[B] Richard the Third, by murdering so many near relations, seemed to
   revenge the sufferings of Henry the Sixth, and his family, on the
   House of York.

V.

"View the stern form that hovers nigh,
  "Fierce rolls his dauntless eye
    "In scorn of hideous death;
"Till starting at a brother's[A] name,
  "Horror shrinks his glowing frame,
    "Locks the half-utter'd groan,
      "And chills the parting breath:--
    "Astonish'd Nature heav'd a moan!
"When her affrighted eye beheld the hands
"She form'd to cherish, rend her holy bands.

[A] Richard the Third, who murdered his brother the Duke of Clarence.

VI.

"Look where a royal infant[A] kneels,
  "Shrieking, and agoniz'd with fear,
  "He sees the dagger pointed near
    "A much-lov'd brother's[B] breast,
"And tells an absent mother all he feels:--
  "His eager eye he casts around;
  "Where shall her guardian form be found,
    "On which his eager eye would rest!
  "On her he calls in accents wild,
  "And wonders why her step is slow
    "To save her suff'ring child!--
"Rob'd in the regal garb, his brother stands
    "In more majestic woe--
  "And meets the impious stroke with bosom bare;

"Then fearless grasps the murd'rer's hands,
    "And asks the minister of hell to spare
    "The child whose feeble arms sustain
    "His bleeding form from cruel Death.--
    "In vain fraternal fondness pleads
        "For cold is now his livid cheek,
    "And cold his last, expiring breath:
        "And now with aspect meek,
    "The infant lifts his mournful eye,
    "And asks with trembling voice, to die,
"If death will cure his heaving heart of pain--
    "His heaving heart now bleeds--
    "Foul tyrant! o'er the gilded hour
    "That beams with all the blaze of power,
        "Remorse shall spread her thickest shroud;
    "The furies in thy tortur'd ear
        "Shall howl, with curses deep, and loud,
    "And wake distracting fear!
        "I see the ghastly spectre rise,
        "Whose blood is cold, whose hollow eyes
        "Seem from his head to start--
        "With upright hair, and shiv'ring heart,
    Dark o'er thy midnight couch he bends,
And clasps thy shrinking frame, thy impious spirit rends."

[A] Richard Duke of York.
[B] Edward the Fifth.

VII.

Now his thrilling accents die--
His shape eludes my searching eye--
But who is he[A], convuls'd with pain,
That writhes in every swelling vein?
  Yet in so deep, so wild a groan,
A sharper anguish seems to live
  Than life's expiring pang can give:--
He dies deserted, and alone--
  If pity can allay thy woes
  Sad spirit they shall find repose--
Thy friend, thy long-lov'd friend is near!
He comes to pour the parting tear,
  He comes to catch the parting breath--
Ah heaven! no melting look he wears,
His alter'd eye with vengeance glares;
Each frantic passion at his soul,
'Tis he has dash'd that venom'd bowl
    With agony, and death.

[A] Sir Thomas Overbury, poisoned in the Tower by Somerset.

VIII.

But whence arose that solemn call?
  Yon bloody phantom waves his hand,
  And beckons me to deeper gloom--
    Rest, troubled form! I come--
  Some unknown power my step impels
  To horror's secret cells--

"For thee I raise this sable pall,
    "It shrouds a ghastly band:
"Stretch'd beneath, thy eye shall trace
    "A mangled regal race:
"A thousand suns have roll'd, since light
"Rush'd on their solid night--
"See, o'er that tender frame grim famine hangs,
    "And mocks a mother's pangs!
"The last, last drop which warm'd her veins
    "That meagre infant drains--
    "Then gnaws her fond, sustaining breast--
    "Stretch'd on her feeble knees, behold
"Another victim sinks to lasting rest--
"Another, yet her matron arms would fold
"Who strives to reach her matron arms in vain--
    "Too weak her wasted form to raise,
    "On him she bends her eager gaze;
    "She sees the soft imploring eye
"That asks her dear embrace, the cure of pain--
    "She sees her child at distance die--
    "But now her stedfast heart can bear
    "Unmov'd, the pressure of despair--
"When first the winds of winter urge their course
"O'er the pure stream, whose current smoothly glides,
"The heaving river swells its troubled tides;
"But when the bitter blast with keener force,
    "O'er the high wave an icy fetter throws,
"The harden'd wave is fix'd in dead repose."--

IX.

"Say who that hoary form? alone he stands,
"And meekly lifts his wither'd hands--
　　"His white beard streams with blood--
"I see him with a smile, deride
"The wounds that pierce his shrivel'd side,
　　"Whence flows a purple flood--
　"But sudden pangs his bosom tear--
　　"On one big drop, of deeper dye,
　　"I see him fix his haggard eye
　"In dark, and wild despair!
"That sanguine drop which wakes his woe--
　　"Say, spirit! whence its source."--
"Ask no more its source to know--
　　"Ne'er shall mortal eye explore
　　"Whence flow'd that drop of human gore,
　"Till the starting dead shall rise,
　"Unchain'd from earth, and mount the skies,
"And time shall end his fated course."--
　"Now th' unfathom'd depth behold--
　　"Look but once! a second glance
　"Wraps a heart of human mold
　　"In death's eternal trance."

X.

"That shapeless phantom sinking slow
"Deep down the vast abyss below,
"Darts, thro' the mists that shroud his frame,
"A horror, nature hates to name!"--

"Mortal, could thine eyes behold
"All those sullen mists enfold,
"Thy sinews at the sight accurst
"Would wither, and thy heart-strings burst;
"Death would grasp with icy hand
"And drag thee to our grizly band--
"Away! the sable pall I spread,
"And give to rest th' unquiet dead--
"Haste! ere its horrid shroud enclose
  "Thy form, benumb'd with wild affright,
"And plunge thee far thro' wastes of night,
  "In yon black gulph's abhorr'd repose!"--
  As starting at each step, I fly,
  Why backward turns my frantic eye,
    That closing portal past?--
Two sullen shades half-seen, advance!--
  On me, a blasting look they cast,
    And fix my view with dang'rous spells,
    Where burning frenzy dwells!--
Again! their vengeful look--and now a speechless--

PERU. A POEM, IN SIX CANTOS.

TO MRS. MONTAGU.

While, bending at thy honour'd shrine, the Muse
  Pours, MONTAGU, to thee her votive strain,
Thy heart will not her simple notes refuse,
  Or chill her timid soul with cold disdain.
O might a transient spark of genius fire
  The fond effusions of her fearful youth;
Then should thy virtues live upon her lyre,
  And give to harmony the charm of truth.
Vain wish! they ask not the imperfect lay,
  The weak applause her trembling accents breathe;
With whose pure radiance glory blends her ray,
  Whom fame has circled with her fairest wreathe.
Thou, who while seen with graceful step to tread
  Grandeur's enchanted round, can'st meekly pause
To rend the veil obscurity had spread
  Where his lone sigh deserted Genius draws;
To lead his drooping spirit to thy fane,
  Where attic joy the social circle warms;
Where science loves to pour her hallow'd strain,
  Where wit, and wisdom, blend their sep'rate charms.
And lure to cherish intellectual powers,
  To bid the vig'rous tides of genius roll,

Unfold, in fair expansion, fancy's flowers,
  And wake the latent energies of soul;
Far other homage claims than flatt'ry brings
  The little triumphs of the proud to grace:
For deeds like these a purer incense springs,
  Warm from the swelling heart its source we trace!
Yet not to foster the rich gifts of mind
  Alone can all thy lib'ral cares employ;
Not to the few those gifts adorn, confin'd,
  They spread an ampler sphere of genuine joy.
While pleasure's lucid star illumes thy bower,
  Thy pity views the distant storm that bends
Where want unshelter'd wastes the ling'ring hour;--
  And meets the blessing that to heav'n ascends!
For this, while fame thro' each successive age
  On her exulting lip thy name shall breathe;
While woman, pointing to thy finish'd page,
  Claims from imperious man the critic wreathe;
Truth on her spotless record shall enroll
  Each moral beauty to her spirit dear;
Paint in bright characters each grace of soul--
  While admiration pours a gen'rous tear.

HELEN MARIA WILLIAMS.

London, April the th, .

ADVERTISEMENT.

That no readers of the following work may entertain expectations respecting it which it would ill satisfy, it is necessary to acquaint them, that the author has not had the presumption even to attempt a full, historical narration of the fall of the Peruvian empire. To describe that important event with accuracy, and to display with clearness and force the various causes which combined to produce it, would require all the energy of genius, and the most glowing colours of imagination. Conscious of her utter inability to execute such a design, she has only aimed at a simple detail of some few incidents that make a part of that romantic story; where the unparalleled sufferings of an innocent and amiable people, form the most affecting subjects of true pathos, while their climate, totally unlike our own, furnishes new and ample materials for poetic description.

THE ARGUMENT.

General description of the country of Peru, and of its animal, and vegetable productions--the virtues of the people--character of Ataliba, **their Monarch--his love for** Alzira--their nuptials celebrated--character of *Zorai,* her father--descent of the genius of Peru--prediction of the fate of that empire.

PERU. CANTO THE FIRST.

Where the pacific deep in silence laves
The western shore, with slow and languid waves,
There, lost Peruvia, rose thy cultur'd scene,
The wave an emblem of thy joy serene:
There nature ever in luxuriant showers
Pours from her treasures, the perennial flowers;
In its dark foliage plum'd, the tow'ring pine
Ascends the mountain, at her call divine;
The palm's wide leaf its brighter verdure spreads,
And the proud cedars bow their lofty heads;
The citron, and the glowing orange spring,
And on the gale a thousand odours fling;
The guava, and the soft ananas bloom,
The balsam ever drops a rich perfume:
The bark, reviving shrub! Oh not in vain
Thy rosy blossoms tinge Peruvia's plain;
Ye fost'ring gales, around those blossoms blow,
Ye balmy dew-drops, o'er the tendrils flow.
Lo, as the health-diffusing plant aspires,
Disease, and pain, and hov'ring death retires;
Affection sees new lustre light the eye,
And feels her vanish'd joys again are nigh.
The Pacos[A], and Vicunnas[B] sport around,
And the meek Lamas[C], burden'd, press the ground.
Amid the vocal groves, the feather'd throng
Pour to the list'ning breeze their native song;

The mocking-bird her varying note essays,
The vain macaw his glitt'ring plume displays.
While spring's warm ray the mild suffusion sheds,
The plaintive humming-bird his pinion spreads;
His wings their colours to the sun unfold,
The vivid scarlet, and the blazing gold;
He sees the flower which morning tears bedew,
Sinks on its breast, and drinks th' ambrosial dew:
Then seeks with fond delight the social nest
Parental care has rear'd, and love has blest:
The drops that on the blossom's light leaf hung,
He bears exulting to his tender young;
The grateful joy his happy accents prove,
Is nature, smiling on her works of love.

  Nor less, Peruvia, for thy favour'd clime
The virtues rose, unsullied, and sublime:
There melting charity, with ardor warm,
Spread her wide mantle o'er th' unshelter'd form;
Cheer'd with the festal song, her lib'ral toils,
While in the lap of age[D] she pour'd the spoils.
Simplicity in every vale was found,
The meek nymph smil'd, with reeds, and rushes crown'd;
And innocence in light, transparent vest,
Mild visitant! the gentle region blest:
As from her lip enchanting accents part,
They thrill with pleasure the reponsive heart;
And o'er the ever-blooming vales around,
Soft echoes waft each undulating sound.

  This happy region *Ataliba* sway'd,
Whose mild behest the willing heart obey'd;
Descendant of a scepter'd, sacred race,

Whose origin from glowing suns they trace;
And as o'er nature's form, the solar light
Diffuses beauty, and inspires delight;
So, o'er Peruvia flow'd the lib'ral ray
Of mercy, lovelier than the smile of day!
In Ataliba's pure and gen'rous heart
The virtues bloom'd without the aid of art.
His gentle spirit, love's soft power possest,
And stamp'd Alzira's image on his breast;
Alzira, form'd each tenderness to prove,
That sooths in friendship, and that charms in love.
But, ah! in vain the drooping muse would paint
(Her accents languid, and her colours faint,)
How dear the joys love's early wishes sought,
How mild his spirit, and how pure his thought,
Ere wealth in sullen pomp was seen to rise,
And break the artless bosom's holy ties;
Blast with his touch affection's op'ning flower,
And chill the hand that rear'd her blissful bower.
Fortune, light nymph! still bless the sordid heart,
Still to thy venal slave thy gifts impart;
Bright in his view may all thy meteors shine,
And lost Peruvia open every mine;
For him the robe of eastern pomp display,
The gems that ripen in the torrid ray;
Collected may their guilty lustre stream
Full on the eye that courts the partial beam:
But Love, oh Love! should haply this late hour,
One softer mind avow thy genuine power;
Breathe at thy altar nature's simple strain,
And strew the heart's pure incense on thy fane;
Give to that bosom scorning fortune's toys,
Thy sweet enchantments, and thy virtuous joys;

Bid pleasure bloom thro' many a circling year,
Which love shall wing, and constancy endear;
Far from this happy clime avert the woes,
The heart from alienated fondness knows;
And from that agony the spirit save,
When unrelenting yawns the op'ning grave;
When death dissolves the ties for ever dear;
When frantic passion pours her parting tear;
With all the cherish'd pains affection feels,
Hangs on the quiv'ring lip, that silence seals;
Views fondness struggling in the closing eye,
And marks it mingling in the falt'ring sigh;
As the lov'd form, while folded to her breast,
On earth's cold bosom seeks more lasting rest!
Leave her fond soul in hopeless griefs to mourn,
Clasp the pale corse, and bathe th' unconscious urn;--
Mild, to the wounds that pierce her bleeding heart,
Nature's expiring pang, and death's keen dart.

   Pure was the lustre of the orient ray,
That joyful wak'd Alzira's nuptial day:
Her auburn hair, spread loosely to the wind,
The virgin train, with rosy chaplets bind;
The scented flowers that form her bridal wreathe,
A deeper hue, a richer fragrance breathe.
The gentle tribe now sought the hallow'd fane,
Where warbling vestals pour'd the choral strain:
There aged Zorai, his Alzira prest
With love parental, to his anxious breast:
Priest of the sun, within the sacred shrine
His fervent spirit breath'd the strain divine;
With glowing hand, the guiltless off'ring spread,
With pious zeal the pure libation shed;

Nor vain the incense of erroneous praise
When meek devotion's soul the tribute pays;
On wings of purity behold it rise,
While bending mercy wafts it to the skies!

  Peruvia! oh delightful land; in vain
The virtues flourish'd on thy beauteous plain;
In vain sweet pleasure there was seen to move,
And wore the smile of peace, the bloom of love;
For soon shall burst the unrelenting storm,
Rend her soft robe, and crush her tender form:
Peruvia! soon the fatal hour shall rise,
The hour despair shall waste in tears and sighs;
Fame shall record the horrors of thy fate,
And distant ages weep for ills so great.

  Now o'er the deep chill night her mantle flung,
Dim on the wave the moon's faint crescent hung;
Peruvia's Genius sought the liquid plain,
Sooth'd by the languid murmurs of the main;
When sudden clamour the illusion broke,
Wild on the surface of the deep it spoke;
A rising breeze expands her flowing veil,
Aghast with fear, she spy'd a flying sail--
The lofty mast impends, the banner waves,
The ruffled surge th' incumbent vessel laves;
With eager eye he views her destin'd foe
Lead to her peaceful shores th' advent'rous prow;
Trembling she knelt, with wild disorder'd air,
And pour'd with frantic energy her pray'r--
"Oh, ye avenging spirits of the deep!
"Mount the blue lightning's wing, o'er ocean sweep;
"Loud from your central caves the shell resound,

"That summons death to your abyss profound;
"Call the pale spectre from his dark abode,
"To print the billow, swell the black'ning flood,
"Rush o'er the waves, the rough'ning deep deform,
"Howl in the blast, and animate the storm--
"Relentless powers! for not one quiv'ring breeze
"Has ruffled yet the surface of the seas--
"Swift from your rocky steeps, ye condors[E] stray,
"Wave your black plumes, and cleave th' aerial way;
"Proud in terrific force, your wings expand,
"Press the firm earth, and darken all the strand;
"Bid the stern foe retire with wild affright,   [F]
"And shun the region veil'd in partial night.
"Vain hope, devoted land! I read thy doom,
"My sad prophetic soul can pierce the gloom;
"I see, I see my lov'd, my favour'd clime,
"Consum'd, and fading in its early prime.
"But not in vain the beauteous realm shall bleed,
"Too late shall Europe's race deplore the deed.
"Region abhorr'd! be gold the tempting bane,
"The curse that desolates thy hostile plain;
"May pleasure tinge with venom'd drops the bowl,
"And luxury unnerve the sick'ning soul."--
Ah, not in vain she pour'd th' impassion'd tear!
Ah, not in vain she call'd the powers to hear!
When borne from lost Peruvia's bleeding land,
The guilty treasures beam'd on Europe's strand;
Each sweet affection fled the tainted shore,
And virtue wander'd, to return no more.

[A] The pacos is a domestic animal of Peru. Its wool resembles the
    colour of dried roses.
[B] The vicunnas are a species of wild pacos.

[C] The lamas are employed as mules, in carrying burdens.

[D] The people cheerfully assisted in reaping those fields, whose produce was given to old persons, past their labour.

[E] The condor is an inhabitant of the Andes. Its wings, when expanded, are said to be eighteen feet wide.

[F Transcriber's note: Misnumbered in original.]

PERU.
CANTO THE SECOND.

THE ARGUMENT.

Pizarro, **a Spanish Captain, lands with his forces--his meeting with**
Ataliba-- **its unhappy consequences** --Zorai **dies** --Ataliba imprisoned,
and strangled --**Alzira's** despair, and madness.

PERU.
CANTO THE SECOND.

Flush'd with impatient hope, the martial band
By stern Pizarro led, approach the land:
No terrors arm the hostile brow, for guile
Charms to betray, in Candour's open smile.
Too artless for distrust, the monarch springs
To meet his latent foe on friendship's wings:
On as he moves, with glitt'ring splendours crown'd,
His feather'd chiefs the golden throne surround;
The waving canopy its plume displays,
Whose varied hues reflect the morning rays;
With native grace he hails the warrior train,

Who stood majestic on Peruvia's plain,
In all the savage pomp of armour drest,
The radiant helmet, and the nodding crest.
Yet themes of joy Pizarro's lips impart,
And charm with eloquence the simple heart;
Unfolding to the monarch's wond'ring thought,
All that inventive arts the rude have taught:
And now he bids the purer spirit rise
Above the circle of surrounding skies;
Presents the page that shed religion's light
O'er the dark mist of intellectual night;
While thrill'd with awe the monarch trembling stands,
He dropp'd the hallow'd volume from his hands.

[A]Sudden, while frantic zeal each breast inspires,
And shudd'ring demons fan the impious fires,
The bloody signal waves, the banners play,
The naked sabres flash their streaming ray;
The martial trumpet's animating sound,
And thund'ring cannon, rend the vault around;
While fierce in sanguine rage the sons of Spain
Rush on Peru's unarm'd, devoted train;
The fiends of slaughter urg'd their dire career,
And virtue's guardian spirits dropp'd a tear.--
Mild Zorai fell, deploring human strife,
And clos'd with prayer his consecrated life.
In vain Peruvia's chiefs undaunted stood,
Shield their lov'd prince, and bathe his robes in blood;
Touch'd with heroic ardor, rush around,
And high of soul, receive each fatal wound:
Dragg'd from his throne, and hurry'd o'er the plain,
The wretched monarch swells the captive train;
With iron grasp, the frantic prince they bear,

And bless the omen of his wild despair.

  Deep in the gloomy dungeon's lone domain,
Lost Ataliba wore the galling chain;
The earth's cold bed refus'd oblivious rest,
While throb'd the pains of thousands at his breast;
Alzira's desolating moan he hears,
And with the monarch's, blends the lover's tears--
Soon had Alzira felt affliction's dart
Pierce her soft soul, and rend her bleeding heart;
Its quick pulsations paus'd, and, chill'd with dread,
A livid hue her fading cheek o'erspread;
No tear she gave to love, she breath'd no sigh,
Her lips were mute, and clos'd her languid eye;
Fainter, and slower heav'd her shiv'ring breast,
And her calm'd passions seem'd in death to rest!--
At length reviv'd, mid rising heaps of slain
She prest with trembling step, the crimson plain;
The dungeon's gloomy depth she fearless sought,
For love, with scorn of danger arm'd her thought:
The cell that holds her captive lord she gains,
Her tears fall quiv'ring on a lover's chains!
Too tender spirit, check the filial tear,
A sympathy more soft, a tie more dear
Shall claim the drops that frantic passion sheds,
When the rude storm its darkest pinion spreads.
Lo! bursting the deep cell where mis'ry lay,
The human vultures seize the dove-like prey!
In vain her treasur'd wealth Peruvia gave,
This dearer treasure from their grasp to save:
Alzira! lo, the ruthless murd'rers come,
This moment seals thy Ataliba's doom.
Ah, what avails the shriek that anguish pours!

The look, that mercy's lenient aid implores!
Torn from thy clinging arms, thy throbbing breast,
The fatal cord his agony supprest:
In vain the livid corse she fondly clasps,
And pours her sorrows o'er the form she grasps--
The murd'rers now their struggling victim tear
From the lost object of her keen despair:
The swelling pang unable to sustain,
Distraction throbb'd in every beating vein:
Its sudden tumults seize her yielding soul,
And in her eye distemper'd glances roll--
"They come! (the mourner cried, with panting breath,)
"To give the lost Alzira rest in death!
"One moment more, ye bloody forms, bestow,
"One moment more for ever cures my woe--
"Lo where the purple evening sheds her light
"On blest remains! oh hide them, pitying night!
"Slow in the breeze I see the verdure wave
"That shrouds with tufted grass, my lover's grave:
"There, on its wand'ring wing in mildness blows
"The mournful gale, nor wakes his deep repose--
"And see, yon hoary form still lingers there!
"Dishevell'd by rude winds his silver hair;
"O'er his chill'd bosom falls the winter's rain,
"I feel the big drops on my wither'd brain:
"Not for himself that tear his bosom steeps,
"For his lost child it flows, for me he weeps!
"No more the dagger's point shall pierce thy breast,
"For calm and lovely is thy silent rest;
"Yet still in dust these eyes shall see thee roll,
"Still the sad thought shall waste Alzira's soul--
"What bleeding phantom moves along the storm?
"It is--it is my lover's well-known form!

"Tho' the dim moon is veil'd, his robes of light
"Tinge the dark clouds, and gild the mist of night:
"Approach! Alzira's breast no terrors move,
"Her fears are all for ever lost in love!
"Safe on the hanging cliff I now can rest,
"And press its pointed pillow to my breast--
"He weeps! in heav'n he weeps! I feel his tear--
"It chills my trembling heart, yet still 'tis dear--
"To him all joyless are the realms above,
"That pale look speaks of pity, and of love!
"My love ascends! he soars in azure light;
"Stay tender spirit--cruel! stay thy flight--
"Again descend in yonder rolling cloud,
"And veil Alzira in thy misty shroud--
"He comes! my love has plac'd the dagger near,
"And on its hallow'd point has dropp'd a tear"--
As roll'd her wand'ring glances wide around
She snatch'd a reeking sabre from the ground;
Firmly her lifted hand the weapon press'd,
And deep she plung'd it in her panting breast:
"'Tis but a few short moments that divide
"Alzira from her love!"--she said--and died.

[A] "Sudden, while frantic zeal, &c." PIZARRO, who during a long
  conference, had with difficulty restrained his soldiers, eager to
  seize the rich spoils of which they had now so near a view,
  immediately gave the signal of assault. At once the martial music
  struck up, the cannon and muskets began to fire, the horse sallied
  out fiercely to the charge, the infantry rushed on sword in hand.
  The Peruvians, astonished at the suddenness of an attack which they
  did not expect, and dismayed with the destructive effects of the
  fire-arms, fled with universal consternation on every side. PIZARRO,
  at the head of his chosen band, advanced directly towards the Inca;

and though his Nobles crowded around him with officious zeal, and
fell in numbers at his feet, while they vied one with another in
sacrificing their own lives, that they might cover the sacred person
of their Sovereign, the Spaniards soon penetrated to the royal seat;
and PIZARRO seizing the Inca by the arm, dragged him to the ground,
and carried him a prisoner to his quarters.-- Robertson's History
of America.

PERU.
CANTO THE THIRD.

THE ARGUMENT.

Pizarro **takes possession of Cuzco--the fanaticism of** Valverde, a Spanish priest--its dreadful effects--A Peruvian priest put to the torture--his daughter's distress--he is rescued by **Las Casas,** an amiable Spanish ecclesiastic, and led to a place of safety, where he dies--his daughter's narration of her sufferings--her death.

PERU.
CANTO THE THIRD.

Now stern Pizarro seeks the distant plains,
Where beauteous Cusco lifts her golden fanes:
The meek Peruvians gaz'd in pale dismay,
Nor barr'd the dark oppressor's sanguine way:
And soon on Cusco, where the dawning light
Of glory shone, foretelling day more bright,
Where the young arts had shed unfolding flowers,
A scene of spreading desolation lowers;
While buried deep in everlasting shade,

Those lustres sicken, and those blossoms fade.
And yet, devoted land, not gold alone,
Or wild ambition wak'd thy parting groan;
For, lo! a fiercer fiend, with joy elate,
Feasts on thy suff'rings, and impels thy fate.
Fanatic fury rears her sullen shrine,
Where vultures prey, where venom'd adders twine;
Her savage arm with purple torrents stains
Thy rocking temples, and thy falling fanes;
Her blazing torches flash the mounting fire,
She grasps the sabre, and she lights the pyre;
Her voice is thunder, rending the still air,
Her glance the livid light'ning's fatal glare;
Her lips unhallow'd breathe their impious strain,
And pure religion's sacred voice profane;
Whose precepts, pity's mildest deeds approve,
Whose law is mercy, and whose soul is love.
Fanatic fury wakes the rising storm--
She wears the stern Valverda's hideous form;
His bosom never felt another's woes,
No shriek of anguish breaks its dark repose.
The temple nods--an aged form appears--
He beats his breast--he rends his silver hairs--
Valverda drags him from the blest abode
Where his meek spirit humbly sought its God:
See, to his aid his child, soft Zilia, springs,
And steeps in tears the robe to which she clings,
Till bursting from Peruvia's frighted throng,
Two warlike youths impetuous rush'd along;
One, grasp'd his twanging bow with furious air,
While in his troubled eye sat fierce despair.
But all in vain his erring weapon flies,
Pierc'd by a thousand wounds, on earth he lies.

His drooping head the heart-struck Zilia rais'd,
And on the youth in speechless anguish gaz'd;
While he, who fondly shar'd his danger, flew,
And from his breast a reeking sabre drew.
"Deep in my faithful bosom let me hide
"The fatal steel, that would our souls divide,"
He quick exclaims--the dying warrior cries,
"Ah, yet forbear!--by all the sacred ties,
"That bind our hearts, forbear"--In vain he spoke,
Friendship with frantic zeal impels the stroke:
"Thyself for ever lost, thou hop'st in vain,
"The youth replied, my spirit to detain;
"From thee, my soul, in childhood's earliest year,
"Caught the light pleasure, and the starting tear;
"Thy friendship then my young affections blest,
"The first pure passion of my infant breast;
"That passion, which o'er life delight has shed,
"By reason cherish'd, and by virtue fed:
"And still in death I feel its strong controul;
"Its sacred impulse wings my fleeting soul,
"That only lingers here till thou depart,
"Whose image lives upon my fainting heart."--
In vain the gen'rous youth, with panting breath,
Pour'd these lost murmurs in the ear of death;
He reads the fatal truth in *Zilia's* eye,
And gives to friendship his expiring sigh.--
But now with rage Valverda's glances roll,
And mark the vengeance rankling in his soul:
He bends his wrinkled brow--his lips impart
The brooding purpose of his venom'd heart;
He bids the hoary priest in mutter'd strains,
Abjure his faith, forsake his falling fanes,
While yet the ling'ring pangs of torture wait,

While yet **Valverda's** power suspends his fate.
"Vain man, the victim cried, to hoary years
"Know death is mild, and virtue feels no fears:
"Cruel of spirit, come! let tortures prove
"The Power I serv'd in life, in death I love."--
He ceas'd--with rugged cords his limbs they bound,
And drag the aged suff'rer on the ground;
They grasp his feeble form, his tresses tear,
His robe they rend, his shrivell'd bosom bare.
Ah, see his uncomplaining soul sustain
The sting of insult, and the dart of pain;
His stedfast spirit feels one pang alone;
A child's despair awakes one suff'ring groan--
The mourner kneels to catch his parting breath,
To sooth the agony of ling'ring death;
No moan she breath'd, no tear had power to flow,
Still on her lip expir'd th' unutter'd woe:
Yet ah, her livid cheek, her stedfast look,
The desolated soul's deep anguish spoke--
Mild victim! close not yet thy languid eyes;
Pure spirit! claim not yet thy kindred skies;
A pitying angel comes to stay thy flight,
Las Casas [A] bids thee view returning light:
Ah, let that sacred drop to virtue dear,
Efface thy wrongs--receive his precious tear;
See his flush'd cheek with indignation glow,
While from his lips the tones of pity flow.
"Oh suff'ring Lord! he cried, whose streaming blood
"Was pour'd for man--Earth drank the sacred flood--
"Whose mercy in the mortal pang forgave
"The murd'rous band, thy love alone could save;
"Forgive--thy goodness bursts each narrow bound,
"Which feeble thought, and human hope surround;

"Forgive the guilty wretch, whose impious hand
"From thy pure altar flings the flaming brand,
"In human blood that hallow'd altar steeps,
"Libation dire! while groaning nature weeps--
"The limits of thy mercy dares to scan,
"The object of thy love, his victim,--Man;
"While yet I linger, lo, the suff'rer dies--
"I see his frame convuls'd--I hear his sighs--
"Whoe'er controuls the purpose of my heart
"First in this breast shall plunge his guilty dart:"
With anxious step he flew, with eager hands
He broke the fetters, burst the cruel bands.
As the fall'n angel heard with awful fear
The cherub's grave rebuke, in grace severe,
And fled, while horror plum'd his impious crest[B],
The form of virtue, as she stood confest;
So fierce Valverda sullen mov'd along,
Abash'd, and follow'd by the guilty throng.
At length the hoary victim, freed from chains,
Las Casas gently leads to safer plains;
Soft Zilia's yielding soul the joy opprest,
She bath'd with floods of tears her father's breast.
Las Casas now explores a secret cave
Whose shaggy sides the languid billows lave;
"There rest secure, he cried, the Christian God
"Will hover near, will guard the lone abode."
Oft to the gloomy cell his steps repair,
While night's chill breezes wave his silver'd hair;
Oft in the tones of love, the words of peace,
He bids the bitter tears of anguish cease;
Bids drooping hope uplift her languid eyes,
And points a dearer bliss beyond the skies.
Yet ah, in vain his pious cares would save

The hoary suff'rer from the op'ning grave;
For deep the pangs of torture pierc'd his frame,
And sunk his wasted life's expiring flame;
To his cold lip Las Casa's hand he prest,
He faintly clasp'd his Zilia to his breast;
Then cried, "the God, whom now my vows adore,
"My heart thro' life obey'd, unknowing more;
"His mild forgiveness then my soul shall prove,
"His mercy share--Las Casa's God, is Love!"
He spoke no more--his Zilia's frantic moan
Was heard responsive to his dying groan.
"Victim of impious zeal, Las Casas cries,
"Accept departed shade, a Christian's sighs;
"And thou, soft mourner, tender, drooping form,
"What power shall guard thee from the fearful storm?
"Weep not for me, she cried, for Zilia's breast
"Soon in the shelt'ring earth shall find its rest.
"Hope not the victim of despair to save,
"I ask but death--I only seek a grave--
"Witness thou mangled form that earth retains,
"Witness a murder'd lover's cold remains.
"I liv'd my father's pangs to sooth, to share;
"I bore to live, tho' life was all despair--
"In vain my lover, urg'd by fond desire
"To shield from torture, and from death my sire,
"Flew to the fane where stern Valverda rag'd,
"And fearless, with unequal force engag'd;
"I saw him bleeding, dying press the ground,
"I drew the poison from each fatal wound;
"I bath'd those wounds with tears--he pour'd a sigh--
"A drop hung trembling in his closing eye--
"Ah, still his mournful sign I shiv'ring hear,
"In every pulse I feel his parting tear--

"I faint--an icy coldness chills each vein,
"No more these feeble limbs their load sustain:
"Spirit of pity! catch my fleeting breath,
"A moment stay--and close my eyes in death--
"*Las Casas*, thee, thy God in mercy gave
"To sooth my pangs--to find the wretch a grave."--
She ceas'd--her spirit fled to purer spheres--
Las Casas bathes the pallid corse with tears--
Fly, minister of good! nor ling'ring shed
Those fruitless sorrows o'er the unconscious dead;
Ah fly--'tis innocence, 'tis virtue bleeds,
And heav'n will listen, when an angel pleads;
I view the sanguine flood, the wasting flame,
I hear a suff'ring world *Las Casas* claim!

[A] LAS CASAS, &c. that amiable Ecclesiastic, who obtained by his
    humanity the title of Protector of the Indies.

[B] --On his crest
    Sat horror plum'd.
                    Par. Lost, iv. .

PERU.
CANTO THE FOURTH.

THE ARGUMENT.

Almagro's expedition to Chili--his troops suffer great hardships from cold, in crossing the Andes--they reach Chili--the Chilese make a brave resistance--the revolt of the Peruvians in Cuzco--they are led on by Manco-Capac, *the successor of* Ataliba-- *his parting with* Cora, his wife--the Peruvians regain half their city *--Almagro* leaves Chili--to avoid the Andes, he crosses a vast desert--his troops can find no water --the rest divide in two bands *--Alphonso* leads the second band, which soon reaches a fertile valley--the Spaniards observe the natives are employed in searching the streams for gold--they resolve to attack them.

PERU.
CANTO THE FOURTH.

Now the stern partner of Pizarro's toils,
Almagro, lur'd by hope of golden spoils,
To distant Chili's ever-verdant meads,

Thro' paths untrod, a band of warriors leads;
O'er the high Andes' frozen steeps they go,
And wander mid' eternal hills of snow:
In vain the vivifying orb of day
Darts on th' impervious ice his fervent ray;
Cold, keen as chains the oceans of the Pole,
Numbs the shrunk frame, and chills the vig'rous soul--
At length they reach luxuriant *Chili's* plain,
Where ends the dreary bound of winter's reign;
Where spring sheds odours thro' th' unvaried year,
And bathes the flower of summer, with her tear.

   When first the brave *Chilese*, with eager glance,
Behold the hostile sons of Spain advance;
Heard the loud thunder of the cannon crash,
And view'd the light'ning of the instant flash,
The threat'ning sabre red with purple streams,
The lance that quiver'd in the solar beams;
With pale surprise they saw the lowring storm,
Where hung dark danger, in an unknown form:
But soon their spirits, stung with gen'rous shame,
Renounce each terror, and for vengeance flame;
Pant high with sacred freedom's ardent glow,
And met intrepid, the superiour foe.
Long unsubdu'd by stern Almagro's train,
Their valiant tribes unequal fight maintain;
Long victory hover'd doubtful o'er the field,
And oft she forc'd Iberia's band to yield;
Oft tore from Spain's proud head her laurel bough,
And bade it blossom on Peruvia's brow;
When sudden tidings reach'd Almagro's ear
That shook the warrior's soul with doubt and fear.

Of murder'd Ataliba's royal race
There yet remain'd a youth of blooming grace,
Who pin'd, the captive of relentless Spain,
And long in Cusco dragg'd her galling chain;
Capac his name, whose soul indignant bears
The rankling fetters, and revenge prepares.
But since his daring spirit must forego
The hope to rush upon the tyrant foe,
Led by his parent orb, that gives the day,
And fierce as darts the keen, meridian ray,
He vows to bend unseen his hostile course,
Then on the victors rise with latent force,
As sudden from its cloud the brooding storm,
Bursts in the thunder's voice, the lightning's form--
For this, from stern Pizarro he obtains
The boon, enlarg'd, to seek the neighb'ring plains,
For one bless'd day, and with his friends unite
To crown with solemn pomp an ancient rite;
Share the dear pleasures of the social hour,
And mid' their fetters twine one festal flower.
So spoke the Prince--far other thoughts possest,
Far other purpose animates his breast:
For now Peruvia's nobles he commands
To lead, with silent step, her martial bands
Forth to the destin'd spot, prepar'd to dare
The fiercest shock of dire, unequal war;
While every tender, human interest pleads,
And urges the firm soul to lofty deeds.
Now Capac hail'd th' eventful morning's light,
Rose with its dawn, and panted for the fight;
But first with fondness to his heart he prest
The tender Cora, partner of his breast;
Who with her lord, had sought the dungeon's gloom,

And wasted there in grief, her early bloom.
"No more, he cried, no more my love shall feel
"The mingled agonies I fly to heal;
"I go, but soon exulting shall return,
"And bid my faithful Cora cease to mourn:
"For oh, amid' each pang my bosom knows,
"What wastes, what wounds it most, are Cora's woes.
"Sweet was the love that crown'd our happier hours,
"And shed new fragrance o'er a path of flowers;
"But sure divided sorrow more endears
"The tie, that passion seals with mutual tears"--
He paus'd--fast-flowing drops bedew'd her eyes,
While thus in mournful accents she replies:
"Still let me feel the pressure of thy chain,
"Still share the fetters which my love detain;
"Those piercing irons to my soul are dear,
"Nor will their sharpness wound while thou art near.
"Oh think not, when in thee alone I live,
"This breast can bear the pain thy dangers give,
"Look on our helpless babe in mis'ry nurst--
"My child--my child, thy mother's heart will burst!
"Methinks I see the raging battle rise,
"And hear this harmless suff'rer's feeble cries;
"I view the blades that pour a sanguine flood,
"And plunge their cruel edge in infant blood."--
She could no more; her falt'ring accents die,
Yet her soul spoke expressive in her eye;
Her lord beholds her grief, with tender pain,
And leads her breathless, to a shelt'ring fane.
Now high in air his feather'd standard waves,
And soon from shrouding woods, and hollow caves,
A num'rous host along the plain appear,
And hail their monarch with a gen'rous tear:

To Cusco's gate now rush th' increasing throngs,
And such their ardor, rouz'd by sense of wrongs,
That vainly would Pizarro's vet'ran force
Arrest the torrent in its raging course;
In vain his murd'ring bands terrific stood,
And plung'd their sabres in a sea of blood;
Danger and death Peruvia's sons disdain,
And half their captive city soon regain.
With such pure joy the natives view their lord
To the warm wishes of their souls restor'd,
As feels the tender child whom force had torn
From his lov'd home, and bruis'd the flower of morn,
When his fond searching eye again beholds
His mother's form, when in her arms she folds
The long lost child, who bathes with tears her face,
And finds his safety in her dear embrace.--

   Soon as Almagro heard applauding fame
The triumphs of Peruvia, loud proclaim,
Unconquer'd Chili's vale he swift forsakes,
And his bold course to distant Cusco takes;
Shuns Andes' icy shower, its chilling snows,
The arrowy gale that on its summit blows;
A burning desart undismay'd he past,
And meets the ardours of the fiery blast.
Now as along the sultry waste they move,
The keenest pang of raging thirst they prove:
No cooling fruit its grateful juice distils,
Nor flows one balmy drop from crystal rills;
For nature sickens in th' oppressive beam,
That shrinks the vernal bud, and dries the stream;
While horror, as his giant stature grows,
O'er the drear void his spreading shadow throws.

Almagro's band now pale, and fainting stray,
While death oft barr'd the sinking warrior's way:
At length the chief divides his martial force,
And bids Alphonso, by a sep'rate course,
Lead o'er the hideous desart half his train--
"And search, he cried, this drear, uncultur'd plain:
"Perchance some fruitage withering in the breeze,
"The pains of lessen'd numbers may appease;
"Or Heav'n in pity, from some genial shower,
"On the parch'd lip one precious drop may pour."

Not far the troops of young Alphonso went,
When sudden, from a rising hill's ascent,
They view a valley, fed by fertile springs,
Which Andes from his lofty summit flings;
Where summer's flowers their mingled odours shed,
And wildly bloom, a waste by beauty spread--
To the charm'd warrior's eye, the vernal scene
That 'mid the howling desart, smil'd serene,
Appear'd like nature rising from the breast
Of chaos, in her infant graces drest;
When warbling angels hail'd the lovely birth,
And stoop'd from heav'n to bless the new-born earth.

And now Alphonso, and his martial band,
On the rich border of the valley stand;
They quaff the limpid stream with eager haste,
And the pure juice that swells the fruitage taste;
Then give to balmy rest the night's still hours,
Fann'd by the sighing gale that shuts the flowers.
Soon as the purple beam of morning glows,
Refresh'd from all their toils, the warriors rose;
And saw the gentle natives of the mead

Search the clear currents for the golden seed;
Which from the mountain's height with headlong sweep
The torrents bear, in many a shining heap--
Iberia's sons beheld with anxious brow
The tempting lure, then breathe th' unpitying vow
O'er those fair lawns to pour a sanguine flood,
And dye those lucid streams with waves of blood.
Thus, while the humming bird in beauty drest,
Enchanting offspring of the ardent West,
Attunes his soothing song to notes of love,
Mild as the murmurs of the mourning dove;
While his soft plumage glows with brighter hues,
And while with tender bill he sips the dews,
The savage Condor, on terrific wings,
From Andes' frozen steep relentless springs;
And quiv'ring in his fangs, his hapless prey
Drops his gay plume, and sighs his soul away.

PERU.
CANTO THE FIFTH.

THE ARGUMENT.

Character of Zamor, *a Bard--his passion for* Aciloe, daughter of the Cazique who rules the valley--the Peruvian tribe prepare to defend themselves--a battle--the Peruvians are vanquished *--Aciloe's* father is made a prisoner, and *Zamor* is supposed to have fallen in the engagement *--Alphonso* becomes enamoured of *Aciloe*-- offers to marry her; she rejects him--in revenge he puts her father to the torture--she appears to consent, in order to save him--meets *Zamor* in a wood --Las Casas *joins them--leads the two lovers to* Alphonso, and obtains their freedom *--Zamor* conducts *Aciloe* and her father to Chili--a reflection on the influence of Poetry over the human mind.

PERU.
CANTO THE FIFTH.

In this sweet scene, to all the virtues kind,
Mild Zamor own'd the richest gifts of mind;
For o'er his tuneful breast the heav'nly muse

Shed from her sacred spring, inspiring dews.
She loves to breathe her hallow'd flame, where art
Has never veil'd the soul, or warp'd the heart;
Where fancy glows with all her native fire,
And passion lives on the exulting lyre.
Nature, in terror rob'd, or beauty drest,
Could thrill with dear enchantment Zamor's breast:
He lov'd the languid sigh the zephyr pours,
He lov'd the murm'ring rill that fed the flow'rs;
But more the hollow sound the wild winds form,
When black upon the billow hangs the storm;
The torrent rolling from the mountain steep,
Its white foam trembling on the darken'd deep--
And oft on Andes' height with eager gaze,
He view'd the sinking sun's reflected rays,
Glow like unnumber'd stars, that seem to rest
Sublime, upon his ice-encircled breast.
Oft his wild warblings charm'd the festal hour,
Rose in the vale, and languish'd in the bower;
The heart's responsive tones he well could move,
Whose song was nature, and whose theme was love.

Aciloe's beauties his fond eye confest,
Yet more Aciloe's virtues warm'd his breast.
Ah stay, ye tender hours of young delight,
Suspend ye moments your impatient flight;
For sure if aught on earth can bliss impart,
Can shed the genuine joy that sooths the heart,
'Tis felt, when early passion's pure controul
Unfolds the first affections of the soul;
Bids her soft sympathies the bosom move,
And wakes the mild emotions dear to love.

The gentle tribe Aciloe's sire obey'd
Who still in wisdom, and in mercy sway'd.
From him the dear illusions long had fled,
That o'er the morn of life enchantment shed;
Yet virtue's calm reflections cheer'd his breast,
And life was joy serene, and death was rest.
Tho' sweet the early spring, her blossoms bright,
When first she swells the heart with pure delight,
Yet not unlovely is the sober ray
That meekly beams o'er autumn's temper'd day;
Dear are her fading beauties to the soul,
While scarce perceiv'd the deep'ning shadows roll.

Now the charm'd lovers dress their future years
In forms of joy, then weep delicious tears,
Expressive on the glowing cheek that hung,
And spoke the fine emotions whence they sprung--
'Twas truth's warm energy, love's sweet controul,
'Twas all that virtue whispers to the soul.
When lo, Iberia's ruthless sons advance,
Roll the stern eye, and shake the pointed lance:
Oh Nature! the destroying band oppose,
Nature, arrest their course--they come thy foes--
Benignant power, where thou with lib'ral care
Hast planted joy, they come to plant despair--
Peruvia's tribe beheld the hostile throng
With desolating fury pour along;
With horror their ensanguin'd path they trac'd,
And now to meet the murd'ring band they haste;
The hoary chief to the dire conflict leads
His death devoted train--the battle bleeds.

Aciloe's searching eye can now no more
The form of Zamor, or her sire explore;
She hears the moan of death in every gale,
She sees a purple torrent stain the vale;
While destin'd all the bitterness to prove
Of mourning duty, and of bleeding love,
Each name that's dearest wakes her bursting sigh,
Throbs at her soul, and trembles in her eye.
Now, pierc'd by wounds, and breathless from the fight,
Her friend, the valiant Omar, struck her sight:
"Omar (she cried) you bleed, unhappy youth,
"And sure that look unfolds some fatal truth:
"Speak, pitying speak, my frantic fears forgive,
"Say, does my father, does my Zamor live?"
"All, all is lost, (the dying Omar said)
"And endless griefs are thine, dear wretched maid;
"I saw thy aged sire a captive bound,
"I saw thy Zamor press the crimson ground"--
He could no more, he yields his fleeting breath,
While all in vain she seeks repose in death.
But, oh, how far each other pang above
Throbs the wild agony of hopeless love;
That grief, for which in vain shall comfort shed
Her healing balm, or time in pity spread
The veil, that throws a shade o'er other care;
For here, and here alone, profound despair
Casts o'er the suff'ring soul a lasting gloom,
And slowly leads her victim to the tomb.

Now rude tumultuous sounds assail her ear,
And soon Alphonso's victor train appear:
Then, as with ling'ring step he mov'd along,
She saw her father mid' the captive throng;

She saw with dire dismay, she wildly flew,
Her snowy arms around his form she threw:
"He bleeds (she cries) I hear his moan of pain,
"My father will not bear the galling chain;
"My tender father will his child forsake,
"His mourning child, but soon her heart will break.
"Cruel Alphonso, let not helpless age
"Feel thy hard yoke, and meet thy barb'rous rage;
"Or, oh, if ever mercy mov'd thy soul,
"If ever thou hast felt her blest controul,
"Grant my sad heart's desire, and let me share
"The load, that feeble frame but ill can bear."

While the young victor, as she falt'ring spoke,
With fix'd attention, and with ardent look,
Hung on her tender glance, that love inspires,
The rage of conquest yields to milder fires.
Yet, as he gaz'd enraptur'd on her form,
Her virtues awe the heart her beauties warm;
And, while impassion'd tones his love reveal,
He asks with holy rites his vows to seal--
"Hop'st thou, she cried, those sacred ties shall join
"This bleeding heart, this trembling hand to thine?
"To thine, whose ruthless heart has caus'd my pains,
"Whose barb'rous hands the blood of Zamor stains!
"Can'st thou--the murd'rer of my peace, controul
"The grief that swells, the pang that rends my soul?
"That pang shall death, shall death alone remove,
"And cure the anguish of despairing love."

 In vain th' enamour'd youth essay'd each art
To calm her sorrows, and to sooth her heart;
While, in the range of thought, her tender breast

Could find no hope, on which her griefs might rest,
While her soft soul, which Zamor's image fills,
Shrinks from the cruel author of its ills.
At length to madness stung by fix'd disdain,
The victor gives to rage the fiery rein;
And bids her sorrows flow from that fond source
Where strong affection feels their keenest force,
Whose breast, when most it suffers, only heeds
The sharper pangs by which another bleeds:
For now his cruel mandate doom'd her sire
Stretch'd on the bed of torture, to expire;
Bound on the rack, unmov'd the victim lies,
Stifling in agony weak nature's sighs.
But oh, what form of language can impart
The frantic grief that wrung Aciloe's heart,
When to the height of hopeless sorrow wrought,
The fainting spirit feels a pang of thought,
Which never painted in the hues of speech,
Lives at the soul, and mocks expression's reach!
At length she trembling cried, "the conflict's o'er,
"My heart, my breaking heart can bear no more--
"Yet spare his feeble age--my vows receive,
"And oh, in mercy, bid my father live!"--
"Wilt them be mine?" the enamour'd chief replies,
"Yes, cruel! see, he dies, my father dies--
"Save, save, my father"--"Dear, angelic maid,
"The charm'd Alphonso cried, be swift obey'd:
"Unbind his chains--Ah, calm each anxious Pain,
"Aciloe's voice no more shall plead in vain;
"Plac'd near his child, thy aged sire shall share
"Our joys still cherish'd by thy tender care"--
"No more (she cried) will fate that bliss allow,
"Before my lips shall breathe the nuptial vow,

"Some faithful guide shall lead his aged feet,
"To distant scenes that yield a safe retreat;
"Where some soft heart, some gentle hand, will shed
"The drops of comfort on his hoary head:
"My Zamor, if thy spirit trembles near,
"Forgive!"--she ceas'd, and pour'd her hopeless tear.

  Now night descends, and steeps each weary breast,
Save sad Aciloe's, in the balm of rest.
Her aged father's beauteous dwelling stood
Near the cool shelter of a waving wood;
But now the gales that bend its foliage die,
Soft on the silver turf its shadows lie;
While, slowly wand'ring o'er the scene below,
The gazing moon look'd pale as silent woe.
The sacred shade, amid whose fragrant bowers
Zamor oft sooth'd with song the evening hours,
Pour'd to the lunar orb, his magic lay,
More mild, more pensive than her musing ray,
That shade with trembling step, the mourner sought,
And thus she breath'd her tender, plaintive thought.
"Ah where, dear object of these piercing pains,
"Where rests thy murder'd form, thy lov'd remains?
"On what sad spot, my Zamor, flow'd the wound
"That purpled with thy streaming blood the ground?
"Oh had Aciloe in that hour been nigh,
"Had'st thou but fix'd on me thy closing eye;
"Told with faint voice, 'twas death's worst pang to part,
"And dropp'd thy last, cold tear upon my heart!
"A pang less bitter then would waste this breast,
"That in the grave alone shall seek its rest.
"Soon as some friendly hand, in mercy leads
"My aged father, safe to Chili's meads;

"Death shall for ever, seal the nuptial tie,
"The heart belov'd by thee is fix'd to die."
She ceas'd, when dimly thro' a flood of tears
She sees her Zamor's form, his voice she hears.--
"'Tis he, she cried, he moves upon the gale,
"My Zamor's sigh is deep--his look is pale--
"I faint"--his arms receive her sinking frame,
He calls his love by every tender name,
He stays her fleeting spirit--life anew
Warms her cold cheek--his tears her cheek bedew--
"Thy Zamor lives, he cried: as on the ground
"I senseless lay, some child of pity bound
"My bleeding wounds, and bore me from the plain--
"But thou art lost, and I have liv'd in vain."
"Forgive, she cried, in accents of despair,
"Zamor forgive thy wrongs, and oh forbear
"The mild reproach that fills thy mournful eye,
"The tear that wets thy cheek--I mean to die!
"Could I behold my aged sire endure
"The pains his wretched child had power to cure?
"Still, still my father, stretch'd in death, I see,
"His grey locks trembling, as he gaz'd on me:
"My Zamor, soft--breathe not so loud a sigh--
"Some list'ning foe may pityless deny
"This parting hour--hark, sure some step I hear,
"Zamor again is lost--for now 'tis near"--
She paus'd, when sudden from the shelt'ring wood
A venerable form before them stood:
"Fear not, soft maid, he cry'd, nor think I come
"To seal with deeper miseries thy doom;
"To bruise the breaking heart that sorrow rends,
"Ah not for this Las Casas hither bends--
"He comes to bid those rising sorrows cease,

"To pour upon thy wounds the balm of peace.
"I rov'd with dire Almagro's ruthless train
"Thro' scenes of death, to Chili's verdant plain;
"Their wish, to bathe that verdant plain in gore,
"Then from its bosom drag the golden ore;
"But mine, to check the stream of human blood,
"Or mingle drops of anguish with the flood.
"When from those fair unconquer'd vales they fled,
"This frame was stretch'd upon the languid bed
"Of pale disease: when helpless, and alone,
"The Chilese spy'd their friend, the murd'rers gone,
"With eager fondness round my couch they drew,
"And my cold hand with gushing tears bedew;
"By day, they sooth my pains with sweet delight,
"And give to watchings the chill hours of night;
"For me their tender spirits joy to prove
"The cares of pity, and the toils of love.
"Soon as I heard, that o'er this gentle scene,
"Where peace and virtue mingled smile serene,
"The foe, like clouds that fold the tempest, hung,
"I hither flew, my breast with anguish wrung.
"A Chilese band the pathless desert trac'd,
"And softly bore me o'er its dreary waste;
"Then parting, at my feet they bend, and clasp
"These aged knees--my soul yet feels their grasp.
"Now o'er the vale with painful step I stray'd,
"And reach'd the shelt'ring grove: there, hapless maid,
"My list'ning ear has caught thy piercing wail,
"My heart has trembled to thy moving tale."--
"And art thou he! the mournful pair exclaim,
"How dear to mis'ry's soul, Las Casas' name!
"Spirit benign, who every grief can share,
"Whose pity stoops to make the wretch its care;

"Weep not for us--in vain thy tear shall flow
"For hopeless anguish, and distracting woe"--
"They ceas'd; in accents mild, the saint returns,
"Yet let me sooth the pains my bosom mourns:
"Come, gentle suff'rers, follow to yon fane,
"Where rests Alphonso, with his victor train;
"My voice shall urge his soul to gen'rous deeds,
"And bid him hear, when truth, and nature pleads."
While in soft tones, Las Casas thus exprest
His pious purpose, o'er Aciloe's breast
A dawning ray of cheering comfort streams,
But faint the hope that on her spirit beams;
Faint, as when ebbing life must soon depart,
The pulse that trembles, while it warms the heart.

   Before Alphonso now the lovers stand;
The aged suff'rer join'd the mournful band;
While with the look that guardian seraphs wear,
When sent to calm the throbs of mortal care,
The story of their woes Las Casas told,
Then cry'd, "the wretched Zamor here behold--
"Hop'st thou, fond man, a passion to controul
"Fix'd in the breast, and woven in the soul?
"But know, mistaken youth, thy power in vain
"Would bind thy victim in the nuptial chain:
"That faithful heart will rend the galling tie,
"That heart will break, that tender form will die--
"Then by each sacred name to nature dear,
"By her strong shriek, her agonizing tear;
"By every horror bleeding passion knows,
"By the wild glance that speaks her frantic woes;
"By all the wasting pangs that rend her breast,
"By the deep groan that gives her spirit rest!

"Let mercy's pleading voice thy bosom move,
"And fear to burst the bonds of plighted love"--
He paus'd--now Zamor's moan Alphonso hears,
Now sees the cheek of age bedew'd with tears:
Palid, and motionless, Aciloe stands,
Fix'd was her mournful eye, and clasp'd her hands;
Her heart was chill'd--her trembling heart, for there
Hope slowly sinks in cold, and dark despair.
Alphonso's soul was mov'd--"No more, he cried,
"My hapless flame shall hearts like yours divide.
"Live, tender spirit, soft Aciloe, live,
"And all the wrongs of mad'ning rage forgive.
"Go from this desolated region far,
"These plains, where av'rice spreads the waste of war;
"Go, where pure pleasures gild the peaceful scene,
"Go where mild virtue sheds her ray serene."

   In vain th' enraptur'd maid would now impart,
The rising joy that swells, that pains her heart;
Las Casas' feet in floods of tears she steeps,
Looks on her sire and smiles, then turns, and weeps;
Then smiles again, while her flush'd cheek, reveals
The mingled tumult of delight she feels.
So fall the crystal showers of fragrant spring,
And o'er the pure, clear sky, soft shadows fling;
Then paint the drooping clouds from which they flow
With the warm colours of the lucid bow.
Now, o'er the barren desert, Zamor leads
Aciloe, and her sire, to Chili's meads:
There, many a wand'ring wretch, condemn'd to roam
By hard oppression, found a shelt'ring home:
Zamor to pity, tun'd the vocal shell,
Bright'ning the tear of anguish, as it fell.

Did e'er the human bosom throb with pain
The heav'nly muse has sought to sooth in vain?
She, who can still with harmony its sighs,
And wake the sound, at which affliction dies;
Can bid the stormy passions backward roll,
And o'er their low-hung tempests lift the soul;
With magic touch paint nature's various scene
Wild on the mountain, in the vale serene;
Can tinge the breathing rose with brighter bloom,
Or hang the sombrous rock in deeper gloom;
Explore the gem, whose pure, reflected ray
Throws o'er the central cave a paler day;
Or soaring view the comet's fiery frame
Rush o'er the sky, and fold the sphere in flame;
While the charm'd spirit, as her accents move,
Is wrapt in wonder, or dissolv'd in love.

PERU.
CANTO THE SIXTH.

THE ARGUMENT.

The troops of Almagro *and* Alphonso *meet on the plains of Cuzco*--
Manco-Capac attacks them by night--his army is defeated, and he is
forced to fly with its scattered remains --*Cora* goes in search of him--
her infant in her arms--overcome with fatigue, she rests at the foot of
a mountain--an earthquake--a band of Indians fly to the mountains for
shelter --Cora discovers her husband--their interview--her death--he
escapes with his infant --*Almagro* claims a share of the spoils of
Cuzco--his contention with *Pizarro*--the Spaniards destroy each other
--Almagro is taken prisoner, and put to death--his soldiers, in revenge,
assassinate *Pizarro* in his palace --*Las Casas* dies --*Gasca,* a
Spanish ecclesiastic, arrives in *Peru*--invested with great power--his
virtuous conduct--the annual festival of the Peruvians--their late
victories over the Spaniards in Chili--a wish for the restoration of
their liberty--the Poem concludes.

PERU.
CANTO THE SIXTH.

At length Almagro, and Alphonso's train,
Each peril past, unite on Cusco's plain:
Capac, who now beheld with anxious woe,
Th' increasing numbers of the powerful foe,
Resolves to pierce beneath the shroud of night
The hostile camp, and brave the vent'rous fight;
Tho' weak the wrong'd Peruvians arrowy showers,
To the dire weapons stern Iberia pours.
Fierce was th' unequal contest, for the soul
When rais'd by some high passion's strong controul,
New strings the nerves, and o'er the glowing frame
Breathes the warm spirit of heroic flame.

But from the scene where raging slaughter burns,
The timid muse with pallid horror turns:
The sounds of frantic woe she panting hears,
Where anguish dims a mother's eye with tears;
Or where the maid, who gave to love's soft power
Her faithful spirit, weeps the parting hour:
And ah, till death shall ease the tender woe,
That soul must languish, and those tears must flow;
For never with the thrill that rapture proves
Shall bless'd affection hail the form she loves;
Her eager glance no more that form shall view,
Her quiv'ring lip has breath'd the last adieu!
Now night, that pour'd upon her hollow gale
The moan of death, withdrew her mournful veil;
The sun rose lovely from the sleeping flood,

And morning glitter'd o'er the field of blood;
Where bath'd in gore, Peruvia's vanquish'd train
Lay cold and senseless on the sanguine plain.
Capac, their gen'rous chief, whose ardent soul
Had sought the rage of battle to controul,
Beheld with keen despair his warriors yield,
And fled indignant from the conquer'd field.
From Cusco now a wretched throng repair,
Who tread mid' slaughter'd heaps in mute despair,
O'er some lov'd corse the shroud of earth to spread,
And drop the sacred tear that sooths the dead:
No shriek was heard, for agony supprest
The fond complaints which ease the swelling breast:
Each hope for ever lost, they only crave
The deep repose which wraps the shelt'ring grave.
So the meek Lama, lur'd by some decoy
Of man, from all his unembitter'd joy;
Ere while, as free as roves the wand'ring breeze,
Meets the hard burden on his bending knees[A];
O'er rocks, and mountains, dark, and waste he goes,
Nor shuns the path where no soft herbage grows;
Till worn with toil, on earth he prostrate lies,
Heeds not the barb'rous lash, but patient dies.
Swift o'er the field of death sad Cora flew,
Her infant to his mother's bosom grew;
She seeks her wretched lord, who fled the plain
With the last remnant of his vanquish'd train:
Thro' the lone vale, or forest's sombrous shade
A dreary solitude, the mourner stray'd;
Her timid heart can now each danger dare,
Her drooping soul is arm'd by deep despair--
Long, long she wander'd, till oppress'd with toil,
Her trembling footsteps track with blood the soil;

In vain with moans her distant lord she calls,
In vain the bitter tear of anguish falls;
Her moan expires along the desert wood,
Her tear is mingled with the crimson flood.

   Where o'er an ample vale a mountain rose,
Low at its base her fainting form she throws;
"And here, my child, (she cried, with panting breath)
"Here let us wait the hour of ling'ring death:
"This famish'd bosom can no more supply
"The streams that nourish life, my babe must die!
"In vain I strive to cherish for thy sake
"My failing strength; but when my heart-strings break,
"When my chill'd bosom can no longer warm,
"My stiff'ning arms no more enfold thy form,
"Soft on this bed of leaves my child shall sleep,
"Close to his mother's corse he will not weep:
"Oh weep not then, my tender babe, tho' near,
"I shall not hear thy moan, nor see thy tear;
"Hope not to move me by thy piercing cry,
"Nor seek with searching look my answering eye."
As thus the dying Cora's plaints arose,
O'er the fair valley sudden darkness throws
A hideous horror; thro' the wounded air
Howl'd the shrill voice of nature in despair;
The birds dart screaming thro' the fluid sky,
And, dash'd upon the cliff's hard surface die;
High o'er their rocky bounds the billows swell,
Then to their deep abyss affrighted fell;
Earth groaning heaves with dire convulsive throws,
While yawning gulphs her central caves disclose:
Now rush'd a frighted throng with trembling pace
Along the vale, and sought the mountain's base;

Purpos'd its perilous ascent to gain,
And shun the ruin low'ring o'er the plain.
They reach'd the spot where Cora clasp'd her child,
And gaz'd on present death with aspect mild;
They pitying paus'd--she lifts her mournful eye,
And views her lord!--he hears his Cora's sigh--
He meets her look--their melting souls unite,
O'erwhelm'd, and agoniz'd with wild delight--
At length she faintly cried, "we yet must part!
"Short are these rising joys--I feel my heart
"My suff'ring heart is cold, and mists arise
"That shroud thy image from my closing eyes:
"Oh save my child!--our tender infant save,
"And shed a tear upon thy Cora's grave"--
The flutt'ring pulse of life now ceas'd to play,
And in his arms a pallid corse she lay:
O'er her dear form he hung in speechless pain,
And still on Cora call'd, but call'd in vain;
Scarce could his soul in one short moment bear
The wild extreme of transport, and despair.

Now o'er the west in melting softness streams
A lustre, milder than the morning beams;
A purer dawn dispell'd the fearful night,
And nature glow'd in all the blooms of light;
The birds awake the note that hails the day,
And spread their pinions in the purple ray;
A zone of gold the wave's still bosom bound,
And beauty shed a placid smile around.
Then, first awaking from his mournful trance,
The wretched Capac cast an eager glance
On his lov'd babe; th' unconscious infant smil'd,
And showers of softer sorrow bath'd his child.

The hollow voice now sounds in fancy's ear,
She sees the dying look, the parting tear,
That sought with anxious tenderness to save
That dear memorial from the closing grave:
He clasps the object of his love's last care,
And vows for him the load of life to bear;
To rear the blossom of a faded flower,
And bid remembrance sooth each ling'ring hour.
He journey'd o'er a dreary length of way,
To plains where freedom shed her hallow'd ray;
O'er many a pathless wood, and mountain hoar,
To that fair clime her lifeless form he bore.
Ye who ne'er suffer'd passions hopeless pain,
Deem not the toil that sooths its anguish vain;
Its fondness to the mould'ring corse extends,
Its faithful tear with the cold ashes blends.
Perchance, the conscious spirit of the dead
Numbers the drops affection loves to shed;
Perchance a sigh of holy pity gives
To the sad bosom, where its image lives.
Oh nature! sure thy sympathetic ties
Shall o'er the ruins of the grave arise;
Undying spring from the relentless tomb,
And shed, in scenes of love, a lasting bloom.
Not long Iberia's sullied trophies wave,
Her guilty warriors press th' untimely grave;
For av'rice, rising from the caves of earth,
Wakes all her savage spirit into birth;
Bids proud Almagro feel her baleful flame,
And Cusco's treasures from Pizarro claim:
Pizarro holds the rich alluring prize,
With firmer grasp, the fires of discord rise.
Now fierce in hostile rage, each warlike train

Purple with issuing gore Peruvia's plain;
There, breathing hate, and vengeful death they flood,
And bath'd their impious bands in kindred blood;
While pensive on each hill, whose lofty brow
O'erhung with sable woods the vale below;
Peruvia's hapless tribes in scatter'd throngs,
Beheld the fiends of strife avenge their wrongs.
Now conquest, bending on her crimson wings,
Her sanguine laurel to Pizarro brings;
While bound, and trembling in her iron chain,
Almagro swells the victor's captive train.
In vain his pleading voice, his suppliant eye,
Conjure his conqu'ror, by the holy tie
That seal'd their mutual league with sacred force,
When first to climes unknown they bent their course;
When danger's rising horrors lowr'd afar,
The storms of ocean, and the toils of war,
The sad remains of wasted life to spare,
The shrivell'd bosom, and the silver'd hair:--
But vainly from his lips these accents part,
Nor move Pizarro's cold, relentless heart,
That never trembled to the suff'rer's sigh,
Or view'd the suff'rer's tear with melting eye.
Almagro dies--the victor's savage pride
To his pale corse funereal rites denied,
Chill'd by the heavy dews of night it lay,
And wither'd in the sultry beam of day,
Till Indian bosoms, touch'd with gen'rous woe,
In the pale form forgot the tyrant foe;
The last sad duties to his ashes paid,
And sooth'd with pity's tear the hov'ring shade.
With unrelenting hate the conqu'ror views
Almagro's band, and vengeance still pursues;

Condemns the victims of his power to stray
In drooping poverty's chill, thorny way;
To pine with famine's agony severe,
And all the ling'ring forms of death to fear;
Till by despair impell'd, the rival train
Rush to the haughty victor's glitt'ring fane;
Swift on their foe with rage impetuous dart,
And plunge their daggers in his guilty heart.
How unavailing now the treasur'd ore
That made Peruvia's rifled bosom poor!
He falls--no mourner near to breathe a sigh,
Catch the last breath, and close the languid eye;
Deserted, and refus'd the holy tear
That warm affection sheds o'er virtue's bier;
Denied those drops that stay the parting breath,
That sooth the spirit on the verge of death;
Tho' now the pale expiring form would buy
With Andes' glitt'ring mines, one faithful sigh!

Now faint with virtue's toil, Las Casas' soul
Sought with exulting hope, her heav'nly goal:
A bending angel consecrates his tears,
And leads his kindred mind to purer spheres.
But, ah! whence pours that stream of lambent light,
That soft-descending on the raptur'd sight,
Gilds the dark horrors of the raging storm--
It lights on earth--mild vision! gentle form--
'Tis Sensibility! she stands confest,
With trembling step she moves, and panting breast;
Wav'd by the gentle breath of passing sighs
Loose in the air her robe expanded flies;
Wet with the dew of tears her soft veil streams,
And in her eye the ray of pity beams;

No vivid roses her mild cheek illume,
Sorrow's wan touch has chas'd the purple bloom:
Yet ling'ring there in tender, pensive grace,
The softer lily fills the vacant place;
And ever as her precious tears bedew
Its modest flowers, they shed a paler hue.
To yon deserted grave, lo swift she flies
Where her lov'd victim, mild Las Casas lies:
Light on the hallow'd turf I see her stand,
And slowly wave in air her snowy wand;
I see her deck the solitary haunt,
With chaplets twin'd from every weeping plant.
Its odours mild the simple vi'let shed,
The shrinking lily hung its drooping head;
A moaning zephyr sigh'd within the bower,
And bent the yielding stem of every flower:
"Hither (she cried, her melting tone I hear
"It vibrates full on fancy's raptur'd ear)
"Ye gentle spirits whom my soul refines,
"Where all its animating lustre shines;
"Ye who can exquisitely feel the glow
"Whose soft suffusion gilds the cloud of woe;
"Warm as the colours varying iris pours
"That tinge with streaming rays the chilling showers;
"Ye to whose yielding hearts my power endears
"The transport blended with delicious tears,
"The bliss that swells to agony the breast,
"The sympathy that robs the soul of rest;
"Hither with fond devotion pensive come,
"Kiss the pale shrine, and murmur o'er the tomb;
"Bend on the hallow'd turf the tear-full eye
"And breathe the precious incense of a sigh.
"Las Casas' tear has moisten'd mis'ry's grave,

"His sigh has moan'd the wretch it fail'd to save!
"He, while conflicting pangs his bosom tear
"Has sought the lonely cavern of despair;
"Where desolate she fled, and pour'd her thought,
"To the dread verge of wild distraction wrought.
"White drops of mercy bath'd his hoary cheek,
"He pour'd by heav'n inspir'd its accents meek;
"In truth's clear mirror bade the mourner's view
"Pierce the deep veil which darkling error drew;
"And vanquish'd empire with a smile resign,
"While brighter worlds in fair perspective shine."--
She paus'd--yet still the sweet enthusiast bends
O'er the cold turf, and still her tear descends;
The ever-falling tears her beauties shroud,
Till slow she vanish'd in a fleecy cloud.

Mild Gasca now, the messenger of peace,
Suspends the storm, and bids the tumult cease.
Pure spirit! in Religion's garb he came,
And all his bosom felt her holy flame;
'Twas then her vot'ries glory, and their care
To bid oppression's harpy talons spare;
To bend the crimson banner he unfurl'd,
And shelter from his grasp a suff'ring world:
Gasca, the guardian minister of woe,
Bids o'er her wounds the balms of comfort flow
While rich Potosi[B] rolls the copious tide
Of wealth, unbounded as the wish of pride;
His pure, unsullied soul with high disdain
For virtue spurns the fascinating bane;
Her seraph form can still his breast allure
Tho' drest in weeds, she triumph'd to be poor--
Hopeless ambition's murders to restrain,

And virtue's wrongs, he sought Iberia's plain,
Without one mean reserve he nobly brings
A massive treasure, yet unknown to kings:
No purple pomp around his dome was spread
No gilded roofs hung glitt'ring o'er his head;
Yet peace with milder radiance deck'd his bower,
And crown'd with dearer joy life's evening hour;
While virtue whisper'd to his conscious heart
The sweet reflexion of its high desert.

  Ah, meek Peruvia, still thy murmur'd sighs
Thy stifled groans in fancy's ear arise;
Sadd'ning she views thy desolated soul,
As slow the circling years of bondage roll,
Redeem from tyranny's oppressive power
With fond affection's force, one sacred hour;
And consecrate its fleeting, precious space,
The dear remembrance of the past to trace.
Call from her bed of dust joy's buried shade;
She smiles in mem'ry's lucid robes array'd,
O'er thy creative scene[C] majestic moves,
And wakes each mild delight thy fancy loves.
But soon the image of thy wrongs in clouds
The fair and transient ray of pleasure shrouds;
Far other visions melt thy mournful eye,
And wake the gushing tear, th' indignant sigh;
There Ataliba's sacred, murder'd form,
Sinks in the billow of oppression's storm;
Wild o'er the scene of death thy glances roll,
And pangs tumultuous swell thy troubled soul;
Thy bosom burns, distraction spreads her flames,
And from the tyrant foe her victim claims.

But, lo! where bursting desolation's night,
A sudden ray of glory cheers my sight;
From my fond eye the tear of rapture flows,
My heart with pure delight exulting glows:
A blooming chief of India's royal race,
Whose soaring soul, its high descent can trace,
The flag of freedom rears on Chili's[D] plain,
And leads to glorious strife his gen'rous train:
And see Iberia bleeds! while vict'ry twines
Her fairest blossoms round Peruvia's shrines;
The gaping wounds of earth disclose no more
The lucid silver, and the glowing ore;
A brighter glory gilds the passing hour,
While freedom breaks the rod of lawless power:
Lo on the Andes' icy steep she glows,
And prints with rapid step th' eternal snows;
Or moves majestic o'er the desert plain,
And eloquently pours her potent strain.
Still may that strain the patriot's soul inspire,
And still this injur'd race her spirit fire.
O Freedom, may thy genius still ascend,
Beneath thy crest may proud Iberia bend;
While roll'd in dust thy graceful feet beneath,
Fades the dark laurel of her sanguine wreath;
Bend her red trophies, tear her victor plume,
And close insatiate slaughter's yawning tomb.
Again on soft Peruvia's fragrant breast
May beauty blossom, and may pleasure rest.
Peru, the muse that vainly mourn'd thy woes,
Whom pity robb'd so long of dear repose;
The muse, whose pensive soul with anguish wrung
Her early lyre for thee has trembling strung;
Shed the weak tear, and breath'd the powerless sigh,

Which soon in cold oblivion's shade must die;
Pants with the wish thy deeds may rise to fame,
Bright on some living harp's immortal frame!
While on the string of extasy, it pours
Thy future triumphs o'er unnumber'd shores.

[A] The Lama's bend their knees and stoop their body in such a manner as
not to discompose their burden. They move with a slow but firm pace,
in countries that are impracticable to other animals. They are neither
dispirited by fasting nor drudgery, while they have any strength
remaining; but, when they are totally exhausted, or fall under their
burden, it is to no purpose to harrass and beat them: they will
continue striking their heads on the ground, first on one side, then
on the other, till they kill themselves,--*Abbe* Raynal's History of
the European Settlements.
[B] See a delightful representation of the incorruptible integrity of
this Spaniard in Robertson's History of America.
[C] "O'er thy creative scene." The Peruvians have solemn days on which
they assume their antient dress. Some among them represent a tragedy,
the subject of which is the death of Atabalipa. The audience, who
begin with shedding tears, are afterwards transported, into a kind of
madness. It seldom happens in these festivals, but that some Spaniard
is slain.--*Abbe* Raynal's *History*.
[D] "On Chili's plain."--An Indian descended from the Inca's, has lately
obtained several victories over the Spaniards, the gold mines have
been for some time shut up; and there is much reason to hope, that
these injured nations may recover the liberty of which they have
been so cruelly deprived.

SONNET,

To MRS. SIDDONS.

Siddons! the Muse, for many a joy refin'd,
  Feelings which ever seem too swiftly fled--
  For those delicious tears she loves to shed,
Around thy brow the wreath of praise would bind--
But can her feeble notes thy praise unfold?
  Repeat the tones each changing passion gives,
  Or mark where nature in thy action lives,
Where, in thy pause, she speaks a pang untold!
When fierce ambition steels thy daring breast,
  When from thy frantic look our glance recedes;
Or oh, divine enthusiast! when opprest
  By anxious love, that eye of softness pleads--
The sun-beam all can feel, but who can trace
The instant light, and catch the radiant grace!

QUEEN MARY'S

COMPLAINT.

I.

Pale moon! thy mild benignant light
May glad some other captive's sight;
Bright'ning the gloomy objects nigh,
Thy beams a lenient thought supply:
But, oh, pale moon! what ray of thine
Can sooth a misery like mine!
Chase the sad image of the past,
And woes for ever doom'd to last.

II.

Where are the years with pleasure gay?
How bright their course! how short their stay!--
Where are the crowns, that round my head
A double glory vainly spread?
Where are the beauties wont to move,
The grace, converting awe to love?
Alas, had fate design'd to bless,
Its equal hand had giv'n me less!

III.

Why did the regal garb array
A breast that tender passions sway?
A soul of unsuspicious frame,
Which leans with faith on friendship's name--
Ye vanish'd hopes! ye broken ties!
By perfidy, in friendship's guise,
This breast was injur'd, lost, betray'd--
Where, where shall Mary look for aid?

IV.

How could I hope redress to find
Stern rival! from thy envious mind?
How could I e'er thy words believe?
O ever practis'd to deceive!
Thy wiles abhorr'd shall please alone
Cold bosoms, selfish as thy own;
While ages hence, indignant hear
The horrors of my fate severe.

V.

Have not thy unrelenting hands
Torn nature's most endearing bands?
Whate'er I hop'd from woman's name,
The ties of blood, the stranger's claim;
A sister-queen's despairing breast
On thee securely lean'd for rest;

On thee! from whom that breast has bled
With sharper ills than those I fled,

VI.

Oh, skill'd in every baser art!
Tyrant! to this unguarded heart
No guilt so black as thine belongs,
Which loads my length'ning years with wrongs.
Strike then at once, insatiate foe!
The long, premeditated blow;
So shall thy jealous terrors cease,
And Mary's harrass'd soul have peace.

EUPHELIA, AN ELEGY.

As roam'd a pilgrim o'er the mountain drear,
  On whose lone verge the foaming billows roar;
The wail of hopeless sorrow pierc'd his ear,
  And swell'd at distance on the sounding shore.

The mourner breath'd her deep complaint to night,
  Her moan she mingled with the rapid blast;
That bar'd her bosom in its wasting flight,
  And o'er the earth her scatter'd tresses cast!

"Ye winds, she cried, still heave the lab'ring deep,
  "The mountain shake, the howling forest rend;
"Still dash the shiv'ring fragment from the steep,
  "Nor for a wretch like me the storm suspend.

"Ah, wherefore wish the rising storm to spare?
  "Ah, why implore the raging winds to save?
"What refuge can the breast where lives despair
  "Desire but death? what shelter but the grave?

"To me congenial is the gloom of night,
  "The savage howlings that infest the air;
"I unappall'd can view the fatal light,
  "That flashes from the pointed lightning's glare.

"And yet erewhile, if night her shadows threw
  "O'er the known woodlands of my native vale;
"Fancy in visions wild the landscape drew,
  "And swelled with boding sounds the whisp'ring gale.

"But deep despair has arm'd my timid soul,
  "And agony has numb'd the throb of fear;
"Taught a weak heart its terrors to controul,
  "And more to court than shun the danger near.

"Yet could I welcome the return of light,
  "Its glim'ring beam might guide my searching eye,
"The sacred spot might then emerge from night,
  "On which a lover's bleeding relicks lie!

"For sure 'twas here, as late a shepherd stray'd
  "Bewilder'd, o'er the mountain's dreary bound,
"Close to the pointed cliff he saw him laid,
  "Where heav'd the waters of the deep around.

"Alas, no longer could his heart endure
  "The woes that heart was doom'd for me to prove:
"He sought for death--for death the only cure,
  "That fate can give to vain, and hopeless love."

"My sire, unjust, while passion swell'd his breast,
  "From the lov'd Alfred his Euphelia tore;
"Mock'd the keen sorrows that my soul opprest,
  "And bade me, vainly bade me love no more!

"He told me love, was like yon' troubled deep,
  "Whose restless billows never know repose;
"Are wildly dash'd upon the rocky steep,

"And tremble to the lightest breeze that blows!

"From these rude storms remote, her gentle balm,
  "Dear to the suff'ring spirit, peace applies"--
Peace! 'tis th' oblivious lake's detested calm
  Whose dull, slow waters never fall or rise.

"Ah, what avails a parent's stern command,
  "The force of conq'ring passion to subdue?
"And wherefore seek to rend, with cruel hand,
  "The ties enchanted love so fondly drew!

"Yet I could see my Alfred's fix'd despair,
  "And aw'd by filial fear conceal my woes;
"My coward heart cou'd separation bear,
  "And check the struggling anguish as it rose!

"'Twas guilt the barb'rous mandate to obey,
  "Which bade no parting sigh my bosom move,
"Victim of duty's unrelenting sway,
  "I seemed a traitor, while a slave to love!"

"Let her, who seal'd a lover's fate, endure
  "The sharpest pressure of deserv'd distress;
"'Twere added perfidy to seek a cure,
  "And stain'd with falsehood, wish to suffer less.

"For wretches doom'd in other griefs to pine,
  "Oft' will benignant hope her ray impart;
"And pity oft' from her celestial shrine,
  "Drop a warm tear upon the fainting heart.

"But o'er the lasting gloom of love's despair,
  "Can hope's bright ray its cheering visions shed?
"Can pity sooth the woes that breast must bear,
  "Which vainly loves, and vainly mourns the dead!"

"No! ling'ring still, and still prolong'd, the moan
  "Shall never pause, till heaves my latest breath,
"Till memory's distracting pang is flown,
  "And all my sorrows shall be hush'd in death.

"And death is pitying come, whose hand shall tear
  "From this afflicted heart the sense of pain;
"My fainting limbs refuse their load to bear,
  "And life no longer will my form sustain.

"Yet once did health's enliv'ning glow adorn,
  "And pleasure shed for me her loveliest ray,
"Pure as the gentle star that gilds the morn,
  "And constant as the equal light of day!"

"Now those lost pleasures trac'd by memory, seem
  "Like yon' illusive meteor's glancing light;
"That o'er the darkness threw its instant gleam,
  "Then sunk, and vanish'd in the depth of night.

"My native vale! and thou delightful bower!
  "Scenes to my hopeless love for ever dear;
"Sweet vale, for whom the morning wak'd her flow'r,
  "Gay bower, for whom the evening pour'd her tear.

"I ask no more to see your beauties rise--
  "Ye rocks and mountains, on whose rugged breast
"My Alfred, murder'd by Euphelia, lies,

"In *your* deep solitudes oh let me rest!"

"And sure the dawning ray that lights the steep,
  "And slowly wanders o'er the purple wave;
"Will shew me where his sacred relics sleep,
  "Will lead his mourner to her destin'd grave.--

O'er the high precipice unmov'd she bent,
  A fearful path the beams of morning shew,
The pilgrim reach'd with toil the rude ascent,
  And saw her brooding o'er the deep below.

"Euphelia stay! he cried, thy Alfred calls--
  "Oh stay, my love! in sorrow yet more dear,
"I come!"--In vain the soothing accent falls,
  Alas, it reach'd not her distracted ear.

"Ah, what avails, she said, that morning rose?
  "With fruitless pain I seek his mould'ring clay;
"Vain search! to fill the measure of my woes,
  "The foaming surge has wash'd his corse away.

"This cruel agony why longer bear?
  "Death, death alone can all my pangs remove;
"Kind death will banish from my heart despair,
  "And when I live again--I live to love!"--

She said, and plung'd into the awful deep--
  He saw her meet the fury of the wave;
He frantic saw! and darting to the steep
  With desp'rate anguish, sought her wat'ry grave.

He clasp'd her dying form, he shar'd her sighs,
  He check'd the billow rushing on her breast;
She felt his dear embrace--her closing eyes
  Were fix'd on Alfred, and her death was blest.--

SONNET,
To EXPRESSION.

Expression, child of soul! I fondly trace
  Thy strong enchantments, when the poet's lyre,
  The painter's pencil catch thy sacred fire,
And beauty wakes for thee her touching grace--
But from this frighted glance thy form avert
  When horrors check thy tear, thy struggling sigh,
  When frenzy rolls in thy impassion'd eye,
Or guilt sits heavy on thy lab'ring heart--
Nor ever let my shudd'ring fancy bear
  The wasting groan, or view the pallid look
  Of him[A] the Muses lov'd--when hope forsook
His spirit, vainly to the Muses dear!
For charm'd with heav'nly song, this bleeding breast,
Mourns the blest power of verse could give despair no rest.--

[A] Chatterton.

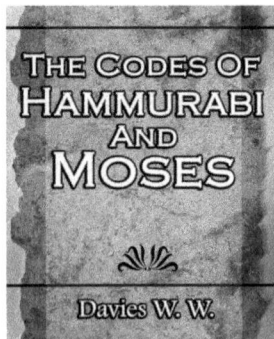

The Codes Of Hammurabi And Moses
W. W. Davies
QTY

The discovery of the Hammurabi Code is one of the greatest achievements of archaeology, and is of paramount interest, not only to the student of the Bible, but also to all those interested in ancient history...

Religion   **ISBN:** *1-59462-338-4*   **Pages:132**
MSRP $12.95

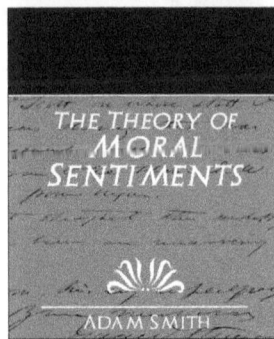

The Theory of Moral Sentiments
Adam Smith
QTY

This work from 1749. contains original theories of conscience amd moral judgment and it is the foundation for systemof morals.

Philosophy **ISBN:** *1-59462-777-0*   **Pages:536**
MSRP $19.95

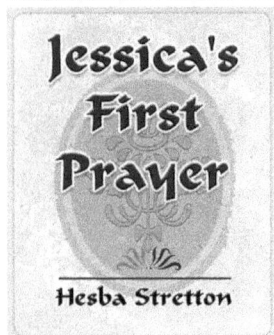

Jessica's First Prayer
Hesba Stretton
QTY

In a screened and secluded corner of one of the many railway-bridges which span the streets of London there could be seen a few years ago, from five o'clock every morning until half past eight, a tidily set-out coffee-stall, consisting of a trestle and board, upon which stood two large tin cans, with a small fire of charcoal burning under each so as to keep the coffee boiling during the early hours of the morning when the work-people were thronging into the city on their way to their daily toil...

Childrens   **ISBN:** *1-59462-373-2*   **Pages:84**
MSRP $9.95

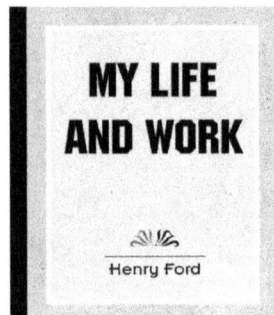

My Life and Work
Henry Ford
QTY

Henry Ford revolutionized the world with his implementation of mass production for the Model T automobile. Gain valuable business insight into his life and work with his own auto-biography... "We have only started on our development of our country we have not as yet, with all our talk of wonderful progress, done more than scratch the surface. The progress has been wonderful enough but..."

Biographies/   **ISBN:** *1-59462-198-5*   **Pages:300**
MSRP $21.95

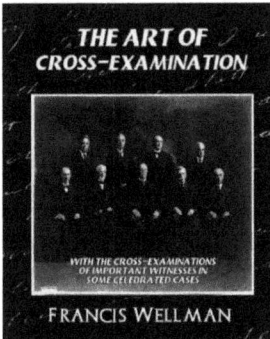

The Art of Cross-Examination
Francis Wellman

QTY

I presume it is the experience of every author, after his first book is published upon an important subject, to be almost overwhelmed with a wealth of ideas and illustrations which could readily have been included in his book, and which to his own mind, at least, seem to make a second edition inevitable. Such certainly was the case with me; and when the first edition had reached its sixth impression in five months, I rejoiced to learn that it seemed to my publishers that the book had met with a sufficiently favorable reception to justify a second and considerably enlarged edition. ...

Pages:412

Reference ISBN: *1-59462-647-2*   *MSRP $19.95*

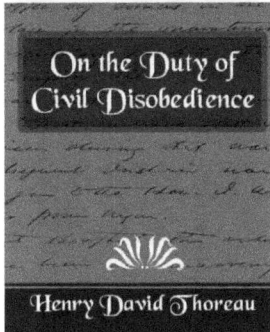

On the Duty of Civil Disobedience
Henry David Thoreau

QTY

Thoreau wrote his famous essay, On the Duty of Civil Disobedience, as a protest against an unjust but popular war and the immoral but popular institution of slave-owning. He did more than write—he declined to pay his taxes, and was hauled off to gaol in consequence. Who can say how much this refusal of his hastened the end of the war and of slavery ?

Law   ISBN: *1-59462-747-9*

Pages:48

MSRP $7.45

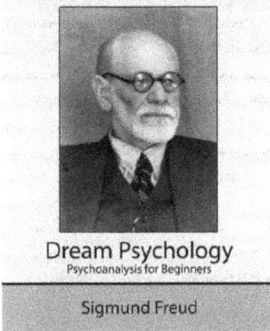

Dream Psychology Psychoanalysis for Beginners
Sigmund Freud

QTY

Sigmund Freud, born Sigismund Schlomo Freud (May 6, 1856 - September 23, 1939), was a Jewish-Austrian neurologist and psychiatrist who co-founded the psychoanalytic school of psychology. Freud is best known for his theories of the unconscious mind, especially involving the mechanism of repression; his redefinition of sexual desire as mobile and directed towards a wide variety of objects; and his therapeutic techniques, especially his understanding of transference in the therapeutic relationship and the presumed value of dreams as sources of insight into unconscious desires.

Pages:196

Psychology ISBN: *1-59462-905-6*   *MSRP $15.45*

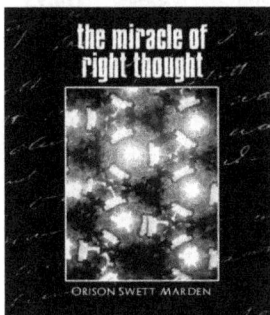

The Miracle of Right Thought
Orison Swett Marden

QTY

Believe with all of your heart that you will do what you were made to do. When the mind has once formed the habit of holding cheerful, happy, prosperous pictures, it will not be easy to form the opposite habit. It does not matter how improbable or how far away this realization may see, or how dark the prospects may be, if we visualize them as best we can, as vividly as possible, hold tenaciously to them and vigorously struggle to attain them, they will gradually become actualized, realized in the life. But a desire, a longing without endeavor, a yearning abandoned or held indifferently will vanish without realization.

Pages:360

Self Help   ISBN: *1-59462-644-8*   *MSRP $25.45*

☐ **The Rosicrucian Cosmo-Conception Mystic Christianity** *by Max Heindel*   ISBN: *1-59462-188-8*   **$38.95**
The Rosicrucian Cosmo-conception is not dogmatic, neither does it appeal to any other authority than the reason of the student. It is: not controversial,
but is: sent forth in the, hope that it may help to clear..   *New Age/Religion Pages 646*

☐ **Abandonment To Divine Providence** *by Jean-Pierre de Caussade*   ISBN: *1-59462-228-0*   **$25.95**
"The Rev. Jean Pierre de Caussade was one of the most remarkable spiritual writers of the Society of Jesus in France in the 18th Century. His death took
place at Toulouse in 1751. His works have gone through many editions and have been republished...   *Inspirational/Religion Pages 400*

☐ **Mental Chemistry** *by Charles Haanel*   ISBN: *1-59462-192-6*   **$23.95**
Mental Chemistry allows the change of material conditions by combining and appropriately utilizing the power of the mind. Much like applied chemistry
creates something new and unique out of careful combinations of chemicals the mastery of mental chemistry...   *New Age Pages 354*

☐ **The Letters of Robert Browning and Elizabeth Barret Barrett 1845-1846 vol II**   ISBN: *1-59462-193-4*   **$35.95**
by Robert Browning and Elizabeth Barrett   *Biographies Pages 596*

☐ **Gleanings In Genesis (volume I)** *by Arthur W. Pink*   ISBN: *1-59462-130-6*   **$27.45**
Appropriately has Genesis been termed "the seed plot of the Bible" for in it we have, in germ form, almost all of the great doctrines which are afterwards
fully developed in the books of Scripture which follow...   *Religion/Inspirational Pages 420*

☐ **The Master Key** *by L. W. de Laurence*   ISBN: *1-59462-001-6*   **$30.95**
In no branch of human knowledge has there been a more lively increase of the spirit of research during the past few years than in the study of Psychology,
Concentration and Mental Discipline. The requests for authentic lessons in Thought Control, Mental Discipline and...   *New Age/Business Pages 422*

☐ **The Lesser Key Of Solomon Goetia** *by L. W. de Laurence*   ISBN: *1-59462-092-X*   **$9.95**
This translation of the first book of the "Lemegton" which is now for the first time made accessible to students of Talismanic Magic was done, after careful
collation and edition, from numerous Ancient Manuscripts in Hebrew, Latin, and French...   *New Age/Occult Pages 92*

☐ **Rubaiyat Of Omar Khayyam** *by Edward Fitzgerald*   ISBN:*1-59462-332-5*   **$13.95**
Edward Fitzgerald, whom the world has already learned in spite of his own efforts to remain within the shadow of anonymity, to look upon as one of the
rarest poets of the century, was born at Bredfield, in Suffolk, on the 31st of March, 1809. He was the third son of John Purcell...   *Music Pages 172*

☐ **Ancient Law** *by Henry Maine*   ISBN: *1-59462-128-4*   **$29.95**
The chief object of the following pages is to indicate some of the earliest ideas of mankind, as they are reflected in Ancient Law, and to point out the
relation of those ideas to modern thought.   *Religion/History Pages 452*

☐ **Far-Away Stories** *by William J. Locke*   ISBN: *1-59462-129-2*   **$19.45**
"Good wine needs no bush, but a collection of mixed vintages does. And this book is just such a collection. Some of the stories I do not want to remain
buried for ever in the museum files of dead magazine-numbers an author's not unpardonable vanity..."   *Fiction Pages 272*

☐ **Life of David Crockett** *by David Crockett*   ISBN: *1-59462-250-7*   **$27.45**
"Colonel David Crockett was one of the most remarkable men of the times in which he lived. Born in humble life, but gifted with a strong will, an
indomitable courage, and unremitting perseverance...   *Biographies/New Age Pages 424*

☐ **Lip-Reading** *by Edward Nitchie*   ISBN: *1-59462-206-X*   **$25.95**
Edward B. Nitchie, founder of the New York School for the Hard of Hearing, now the Nitchie School of Lip-Reading, Inc, wrote "LIP-READING Principles
and Practice". The development and perfecting of this meritorious work on lip-reading was an undertaking...   *How-to Pages 400*

☐ **A Handbook of Suggestive Therapeutics, Applied Hypnotism, Psychic Science**   ISBN: *1-59462-214-0*   **$24.95**
by Henry Munro   *Health/New Age/Health/Self-help Pages 376*

☐ **A Doll's House: and Two Other Plays** *by Henrik Ibsen*   ISBN: *1-59462-112-8*   **$19.95**
Henrik Ibsen created this classic when in revolutionary 1848 Rome. Introducing some striking concepts in playwriting for the realist genre, this play
has been studied the world over.   *Fiction/Classics/Plays 308*

☐ **The Light of Asia** *by sir Edwin Arnold*   ISBN: *1-59462-204-3*   **$13.95**
In this poetic masterpiece, Edwin Arnold describes the life and teachings of Buddha. The man who was to become known as Buddha to the world was
born as Prince Gautama of India but he rejected the worldly riches and abandoned the reigns of power when... Religion/History/Biographies Pages 170

☐ **The Complete Works of Guy de Maupassant** *by Guy de Maupassant*   ISBN: *1-59462-157-8*   **$16.95**
"For days and days, nights and nights, I had dreamed of that first kiss which was to consecrate our engagement, and I knew not on what spot I should
put my lips..."   *Fiction/Classics Pages 240*

☐ **The Art of Cross-Examination** *by Francis L. Wellman*   ISBN: *1-59462-309-0*   **$26.95**
Written by a renowned trial lawyer, Wellman imparts his experience and uses case studies to explain how to use psychology to extract desired information
through questioning.   *How-to/Science/Reference Pages 408*

☐ **Answered or Unanswered?** *by Louisa Vaughan*   ISBN: *1-59462-248-5*   **$10.95**
Miracles of Faith in China   *Religion Pages 112*

☐ **The Edinburgh Lectures on Mental Science (1909)** *by Thomas*   ISBN: *1-59462-008-3*   **$11.95**
This book contains the substance of a course of lectures recently given by the writer in the Queen Street Hall, Edinburgh. Its purpose is to indicate the
Natural Principles governing the relation between Mental Action and Material Conditions...   *New Age/Psychology Pages 148*

☐ **Ayesha** *by H. Rider Haggard*   ISBN: *1-59462-301-5*   **$24.95**
Verily and indeed it is the unexpected that happens! Probably if there was one person upon the earth from whom the Editor of this, and of a certain previ-
ous history, did not expect to hear again...   *Classics Pages 380*

☐ **Ayala's Angel** *by Anthony Trollope*   ISBN: *1-59462-352-X*   **$29.95**
The two girls were both pretty, but Lucy who was twenty-one who supposed to be simple and comparatively unattractive, whereas Ayala was credited, as
her Bombwhat romantic name might show, with poetic charm and a taste for romance. Ayala when her father died was nineteen...   Fiction Pages 484

☐ **The American Commonwealth** *by James Bryce*   ISBN: *1-59462-286-8*   **$34.45**
An interpretation of American democratic political theory. It examines political mechanics and society from the perspective of Scotsman
James Bryce   *Politics Pages 572*

☐ **Stories of the Pilgrims** *by Margaret P. Pumphrey*   ISBN: *1-59462-116-0*   **$17.95**
This book explores pilgrims religious oppression in England as well as their escape to Holland and eventual crossing to America on the Mayflower, and
their early days in New England...   *History Pages 268*

www.bookjungle.com *email: sales@bookjungle.com fax: 630-214-0564 mail: Book Jungle PO Box 2226 Champaign, IL 61825*

QTY

The Fasting Cure *by Sinclair Upton*   ISBN: *1-59462-222-1* **$13.95**
In the Cosmopolitan Magazine for May, 1910, and in the Contemporary Review (London) for April, 1910, I published an article dealing with my experiences in fasting. I have written a great many magazine articles, but never one which attracted so much attention... New Age/Self Help/Health Pages 164

Hebrew Astrology *by Sepharial*   ISBN: *1-59462-308-2* **$13.45**
In these days of advanced thinking it is a matter of common observation that we have left many of the old landmarks behind and that we are now pressing forward to greater heights and to a wider horizon than that which represented the mind-content of our progenitors...   Astrology Pages 144

Thought Vibration or The Law of Attraction in the Thought World   ISBN: *1-59462-127-6* **$12.95**
by William Walker Atkinson   *Psychology/Religion Pages 144*

Optimism *by Helen Keller*   ISBN: *1-59462-108-X* **$15.95**
Helen Keller was blind, deaf, and mute since 19 months old, yet famously learned how to overcome these handicaps, communicate with the world, and spread her lectures promoting optimism. An inspiring read for everyone...   Biographies/Inspirational Pages 84

Sara Crewe *by Frances Burnett*   ISBN: *1-59462-360-0* **$9.45**
In the first place, Miss Minchin lived in London. Her home was a large, dull, tall one, in a large, dull square, where all the houses were alike, and all the sparrows were alike, and where all the door-knockers made the same heavy sound...   Childrens/Classic Pages 88

The Autobiography of Benjamin Franklin *by Benjamin Franklin*   ISBN: *1-59462-135-7* **$24.95**
The Autobiography of Benjamin Franklin has probably been more extensively read than any other American historical work, and no other book of its kind has had such ups and downs of fortune. Franklin lived for many years in England, where he was agent...   Biographies/History Pages 332

Name	
Email	
Telephone	
Address	
City, State ZIP	

☐ **Credit Card**   ☐ **Check / Money Order**

Credit Card Number	
Expiration Date	
Signature	

Please Mail to: Book Jungle
PO Box 2226
Champaign, IL 61825
or Fax to: 630-214-0564

ORDERING INFORMATION
web: *www.bookjungle.com*
email: *sales@bookjungle.com*
fax: *630-214-0564*
mail: *Book Jungle PO Box 2226 Champaign, IL 61825*
or PayPal *to sales@bookjungle.com*

Please contact us for bulk discounts

DIRECT-ORDER TERMS

20% Discount if You Order Two or More Books
Free Domestic Shipping!
Accepted: Master Card, Visa, Discover, American Express

www.ingramcontent.com/pod-product-compliance
Lightning Source LLC
Chambersburg PA
CBHW080532090426
42733CB00015B/2564

9 781438 527093